Lectionary Worship Aids

Series VII, Cycle C

Frank Ramirez

CSS Publishing Company, Inc., Lima, Ohio

LECTIONARY WORSHIP AIDS, SERIES VII, CYCLE C

Library of Congress Cataloging-in-Publication Data

Ramirez, Frank, 1954-
Lectionary worship aids. Series VII / Frank Ramirez.
p. cm.
ISBN 0-7880-2317-9 (alk. paper)
1. Worship programs. 2. Common lectionary (1992), I. Title.

BV198.R29 2004
264—dc22

2004008728

For more information about CSS Publishing Company resources, visit our website at www.csspub.com or email us at custserv@csspub.com or call (800) 241-4056.

Cover design by Chris Patton/Barbara Spencer
ISBN 0-7880-2404-3

PRINTED IN U.S.A.

To Dec and Lois Gowans,
who hosted the two of us in 1977
when Jennie and I accepted the assignment
for me to serve as summer pastor
at the Modesto Church of the Brethren.
Hopefully your prayers for us
that summer were answered!

Table Of Contents

Easter Season

Season Of Pentecost

Introduction

This is the third of three books of lectionary prayers I've written for this series. It's been fun, and one of the biggest challenges has been to constantly remind myself that this is not an academic exercise of matching themes with various scriptures. These are not words to be admired. They are words to be prayed. This is all about talking to God. Just as importantly, it's about listening to God talking back.

On more than one occasion in this volume I have tried to leave at least a little space for listening. I hope that people use times of silence, both in worship and in life, to allow the opportunity for God to speak.

There is, of course, no controlling God. We cannot pull on a chain and ensure a reply. That would be magic. But we can at least work on the assumption that prayer is a conversation, not a one-way harangue, part medical report and part Santa wish list. We can also work on the assumption that this is the Lord of the universe we are speaking to, awe-inspiring and majestic, yet somehow marvelously secure as a God who encourages us to speak on an intimate basis. When we follow the example of Jesus and address God as "Abba," we have gone beyond *Father* to *Daddy.*

This volume is intended as a guide for worship planners, to provide words for worship leaders, and for congregational prayer. In many instances, words are taken directly from scripture (we can hardly argue with the source) or are paraphrased in order to suit the occasion of unison rather than individual prayer. In these cases, I have always tried to identify the text, and if I have forgotten to make such an identification I appreciate your kindness and understanding.

I have also, as with the previous two volumes, included some additional resources at the end of the book including prayers, original hymn texts to go with familiar tunes, and a few hymns from my own tradition, that of the Church of the Brethren, which are in the public domain. Copies can be made.

I want to thank the staff at CSS Publishing Company for their confidence in me, hopefully not misplaced. I've enjoyed this assignment immensely, and as always I can continue to say truthfully that I have always depended on the kindness of editors.

Even with aids such as the present volume contains along with many others from CSS it would be surprising if we weren't occasionally tongue-tied when addressing God. On those occasions, I would suggest, rather than engage in endless repetition to fill space, what we call "vamping" in the theater, that we consider the words of Romans 8:26-27. If all else fails simply remember that the Apostle Paul said: "Likewise the Spirit helps us in our weakness; for we do not know how to pray as we ought, but that very Spirit intercedes with sighs too deep for words. And God, who searches the heart, knows what is the mind of the Spirit, because the Spirit intercedes for the saints according to the will of God."

The idea for the service contained in the First Lesson for Ash Wednesday has its source in an idea developed by Reverend Dick Williams of the Everett United Methodist Church for a joint service held in 2005. We shared the Ash Wednesday Service with our Methodist cousins, and they joined us Brethren for our Love Feast on Maundy Thursday.

The Service for Hunters contained in Special Services might strike some as a little odd. I have never gone hunting, nor have I ever fired a gun. However, when I moved to Everett, Pennsylvania, I was struck by how much hunting was a way of connecting people with God's creation. The deer have no natural enemy other than the front grille of cars and trucks. The herd gets diseased when it experiences no culling, and herds can destroy forests and their habitats for other creatures when the deer population gets out of control.

Hunters here eat what they kill. They share the meat with shelters and food pantries, as well as friends and family. The hunt is shared by men and women across several generations. I wanted to honor that spirit and connect it to God's call to care for creation, so I have developed a new service for hunters each year. There are several seasons in this area, but the big one is Buck Season, which begins the Monday after Thanksgiving. It is a holiday. The schools and many businesses are closed. We have the service during worship the day before.

Frank Ramirez
Everett, Pennsylvania
Christmas 2005

First Sunday Of Advent

First Lesson: Jeremiah 33:14-16
Theme: Empires Come And Go — God Lasts

Call To Worship (Psalm 25:14)

The friendship of the Lord is for those who fear him, and he makes his covenant known to them.

Collect

O come, Immanuel, come, Lord Jesus, into our hearts this Advent season. Let the day come, Lord, when you will perform that good thing you have promised to us, when you shall execute judgment and righteousness in the land. You, Lord, are our righteousness. In you we are made one. In you we are made whole. Behold, the days come when we shall see the light. Guard us all together and bring us to that place. Amen.

Prayer Of Confession

Immanuel, God with us, call to us we pray, especially when we are tempted to stray, to compromise with the world. Amen.

Hymns

O Come, O Come, Emmanuel
There's A Song In The Air
Great God Of Wonders

First Sunday Of Advent

Second Lesson: 1 Thessalonians 3:9-13
Theme: Night And Day

Call To Worship (based on Psalm 25:1-5)

One: To you, O Lord, we lift up our souls.

All: In you, our God, we put our trust.

One: Help us to know your ways, O Lord; teach us your paths.

All: Lead us in your truth, and teach us, for you are the God of our salvation; for you we wait all day long.

Collect

Night and day your glories are revealed. Day and night your presence is proven. As we gather in your name we profess that name, and wear that name, strengthen our love for you. Amen.

Prayer Of Confession

This day, Lord, we have heard your voice in our midst, and we lift up to you now our sins as well as our confession of faith in your forgiveness. Bless us as your family as we seek to minister to each other, and to the world. Amen.

Hymns

Soon And Very Soon
Good Night And Good Morning
The Lord Bless You And Keep You

First Sunday Of Advent

Gospel Lesson: Luke 21:25-36
Theme: God Is Near Again

Call To Worship

There will be signs in the sun, moon, and stars,
And nations confounded infested by wars.
The Son of Man is coming in glory
And that is only half of the story.
"Look at the trees, and the time of the year.
The trial is coming! You've nothing to fear!
Be alert at all times, and for strength you must pray.
Heaven and earth are passing away."
But God on his throne, and the bright, living Word
Will triumph in spite of both fire and sword.

Collect

Lord Jesus, we gather in your name, prepared to wait, to listen, to hear you. Our redemption draws nigh, and with your heart we pray that we might see your salvation as one people acknowledging one Lord. Inspire to us make straight your paths, to level all obstacles that keep people from gathering in your name. These things we pray in hope and expectation. Amen.

Prayer Of Confession

Lord in heaven, as we prepare for the gift of your Son, touch our hearts that we may continue to prepare our gifts for your needy, your children, your poor, and your outcasts, near at hand and around the world. Amen.

Hymns

Let All Mortal Flesh Keep Silence
All The World Is Sleeping *(see page 265)*
Jesus Came — The Heavens Adoring

Second Sunday Of Advent

First Lesson: Malachi 3:1-4
Theme: My Messenger

Call To Worship (based on Malachi 3:1-4)

Lord of this season and every season, we see that you are sending a messenger to prepare the way for the Lord. We know the messenger of the covenant is the one in whom you delight! Yet we wonder, with all the trappings of the season, all the distractions, and our exhaustion and expectations, who can endure the day of your coming, and who can stand when you appear? We praise you because you are like a refiner and purifier of silver. We count on you to purify us until we can present to you a perfect sacrifice of righteousness, this praise we offer up today. May our lives be pleasing to you as in the days of old and in former years. Amen.

Collect

Send us, O Lord, to warn your sleeping people. Goad us, and guide us, grant us time enough to proclaim that if we are tested then with your strengthening, we may prove pure as gold in your service. Amen.

Prayer Of Confession

We give of ourselves to your kingdom, seeking no return, save the knowledge that you are the first giver, the best giver, who will be able to take our lives and from our humble confession fashion a vessel of obedience. Bless us this day. Amen.

Hymns

Come, Now Is The Time To Worship
Spirit Of The Living God
Here I Am, Lord

Second Sunday Of Advent

Second Lesson: Philippians 1:3-11
Theme: Blessed Be The Lord!

Call To Worship (based on Isaiah 40:3-8)

One: Prepare ye the way of the Lord.
All: A voice cries out: "In the wilderness prepare the way of the Lord, make straight in the desert a highway for our God.
One: Prepare ye the way of the Lord.
All: Every valley shall be lifted up, and every mountain and hill be made low; the uneven ground shall become level, and the rough places a plain.
One: Prepare ye the way of the Lord.
All: Then the glory of the Lord shall be revealed, and all people shall see it together, for the mouth of the Lord has spoken."
One: Prepare ye the way of the Lord.
All: A voice says, "Cry out!" And I said, "What shall I cry?" All people are grass, their constancy is like the flower of the field.
One: Prepare ye the way of the Lord.
All: The grass withers, the flower fades, when the breath of the Lord blows upon it; surely the people are grass.
One: Prepare ye the way of the Lord.
All: The grass withers, the flower fades; but the Word of our God will stand forever.

Collect (based on Philippians 1:9-11)

Lord, hear our prayer, that your love may overflow more and more with knowledge and full insight to help us to determine what is best, so that in the day of Christ we may be pure and blameless, having produced the harvest of righteousness that comes through Jesus Christ for your glory and praise. Amen.

Prayer Of Confession

God of Advent, we do not always pray with the joy we are promised. We do not always act out of faith, but out of fear. Call us beyond our doubts to claim the hope eternal that you have granted to your pilgrim people. In your name we pray. Amen.

Hymns

Majesty
O Come, All Ye Faithful
Go Tell It On The Mountain

Second Sunday Of Advent

Gospel Lesson: Luke 3:1-6
Theme: Get Ready For God

Call To Worship

From out of the desert, the voice of one crying,
As prophets once perched in the past had foretold
And all who are curious come to see trying
To look past the sackcloth and hear the Lord's Word.

Collect

Lord, you prepare a way for us in the wilderness. We strive to prepare a place for you in our hearts. In the midst of distraction and confusion we gather to praise you, proclaim our love for you and for each other, and commit ourselves to your service in all things. Your Word stands forever. Your glory is revealed. Amen.

Prayer Of Confession

Lord, hear our prayers. Hear what we say, and what we do not say as well. Allow us to mirror, if only imperfectly, your perfect compassion in all we say and do. Allow us to extend the grace to others that you have extended to us. Bless us and make clear for us the opportunities for ministry to each other that have been revealed in our worship together. These things we pray in the name of the infant Jesus, who is revealed to us in this season. Amen.

Hymns

O Come, All Ye Faithful
While All Around The Bells May Ring *(see page 266)*
Bless'd Be The God Of Israel

Third Sunday Of Advent

First Lesson: Zephaniah 3:14-20
Theme: Even So!

Call To Worship (Zephaniah 3:15)

The Lord has taken away the judgments against you, he has turned away your enemies. The king of Israel, the Lord, is in your midst; you shall fear disaster no more.

Collect

Renew us, O God, as in the best of times when your people return to your Word. Turn back those things which are obstacles in our lives as we walk a straight path toward your salvation. Amen.

Prayer Of Confession

Renewing God, we take stock of all the ways we have fallen short. We call to mind the misfortunes that are not our fault. We struggle to forget the sins of others. Even so, we will shout aloud, for you have not abandoned us, and in calling us to mind you have sent us a Savior — Christ the Lord! Amen.

Hymns

Comfort, Comfort, O My People
Come, Thou Long Expected Jesus
Hark To The Lord's Anointed

Third Sunday Of Advent

Second Lesson: Philippians 4:4-7
Theme: Say It Again!

Call To Worship (Philippians 4:4-8)

One: Rejoice in the Lord always; again I will say, Rejoice.

All: Let your gentleness be known to everyone. The Lord is near.

One: Do not worry about anything, but in everything by prayer and supplication with thanksgiving let your requests be made known to God.

All: And the peace of God, which surpasses all understanding, will guard your hearts and your minds in Christ Jesus.

One: Finally, beloved,

All: whatever is true, whatever is honorable, whatever is just, whatever is pure, whatever is pleasing, whatever is commendable, if there is any excellence and if there is anything worthy of praise, think about these things.

Collect

Let our rejoicing be continuous, God of salvation. Hear our call as we recognize and claim what is true, honorable, just, pure, pleasing, commendable, excellent, and worthy of praise, for they all have their source in you. Amen.

Prayer Of Confession

What joy is ours, God of many gifts. What joy we have denied by focusing on the negative in our lives together. Call us to think upon those things which demonstrate your presence among us, and away from barriers that keep us apart. Come, Lord Jesus, return to us now that we need you most. Amen.

Hymns

Sweet Hour Of Prayer
Lord, With Devotion We Pray
Rejoice, The Lord Is King!

Third Sunday Of Advent

Gospel Lesson: Luke 3:7-18
Theme: Fruits Worthy Of Repentance

Call To Worship (Isaiah 12:2-6)

One: Surely God is my salvation; I will trust, and will not be afraid, for the Lord God is my strength and my might; he has become my salvation.

All: With joy you will draw water from the wells of salvation.

One: And you will say in that day: Give thanks to the Lord, call on his name; make known his deeds among the nations; proclaim that his name is exalted.

All: Sing praises to the Lord, for he has done gloriously; let this be known in all the earth. Shout aloud and sing for joy, O royal Zion, for great in your midst is the Holy One of Israel.

Collect

Lord, we remember on this Third Sunday Of Advent that you are the source of our celebration. We call upon your name. We are not afraid. You are our strength when we are weak. You are our words when we struggle to express your goodness. You are our Spirit when our own will is struggling. Bless us in our gathering and in our departing today. These things we pray in the name of your Son and our Savior, Jesus Christ. Amen.

Prayer Of Confession

Lord of judgment, God of mercy, you call us to account, you call us to task, and you call us to higher things. So often we focus on what is not important. Today in prayer and supplication we give you thanks and lift up our requests to you. Grant us the peace which passes all understanding, and guard our hearts and minds in Christ Jesus. Amen.

Hymns

It Came Upon A Midnight Clear
Hark! The Glad Song
A Hymn For Anointing *(see page 267)*

Fourth Sunday Of Advent

First Lesson: Micah 5:2-5a
Theme: Can So

Call To Worship (Psalm 80:7)

Restore us, O God of hosts; let your face shine, that we may be saved.

Collect

God of peace, we pray for your presence in our congregation today as we seek to speak your Word against the clamor of a distracting, yet hurting, world. Amen.

Prayer Of Confession

Lord, it was nothing to you to bypass Jerusalem and call your Savior out of Bethlehem (house of bread). And it is just as likely that you will call forth another prophet from our midst. We pledge to open our hearts to your leading for our lives, and to judge one another not based on our preconceptions, but according to the measure of the gifts your Holy Spirit has granted to us. We pray these things in your name. Amen.

Hymns

Good Christian Friends, Rejoice
O Come, All Ye Faithful
Joy To The World

Fourth Sunday Of Advent

Second Lesson: Hebrews 10:5-10
Theme: This Day

Call To Worship

We have come, not to offer the sacrifice of a moment, but to do God's will, this day in worship, that our days may become worship.

Collect

Lord, we stand on the edge of the great news of our Savior's birth. While the world demands, we rush, you tell us to bide. While the world tells us to buy, you ask us to wait. While the world insists, we cross one item after another off our to-do lists, you simply advise us to be ready. With your help we intend to let your blessings come to pass at a time and place of your choosing. This moment we cast away our cares and concerns, and come to adore you. These things we pray in the name of the infant Jesus. Amen.

Prayer Of Confession

Will. What we will. What we won't. What we ought. What we don't. Will. God's will. God, let your will be done as one in our lives together that we may gather as one body, one will. Yours. Amen.

Hymns

Angels We Have Heard On High
Away In A Manger (The Cradle Song)
While Shepherds Watched

Fourth Sunday Of Advent

Gospel Lesson: Luke 1:39-45 (46-55)
Theme: Looks Big To Me

Call To Worship (Micah 5:2-5a)

One: But you, O Bethlehem of Ephrathah, who are one of the little clans of Judah, from you shall come forth for me one who is to rule in Israel, whose origin is from of old, from ancient days.

All: Therefore he shall give them up until the time when she who is in labor has brought forth; then the rest of his kindred shall return to the people of Israel.

One: And he shall stand and feed his flock in the strength of the Lord, in the majesty of the name of the Lord his God. And they shall live secure, for now he shall be great to the ends of the earth;

All: and he shall be the one of peace.

Collect

Magnify, Lord, our souls today that we might reflect your patience and your pleading, that the world might be saved through you. Amen.

Prayer Of Confession

God who favors the oppressed, we confess that our economic state puts us on the wrong side of your historical equation. You have come to vindicate the lowly, and to raise up those who have been brought low by the world's pain. May we, as did your Son, humble ourselves for the salvation of the whole world, in this time and in the world to come. Amen.

Hymns

The First Noel
Gabriel's Message
What Child Is This?

Christmas Eve

First Lesson: Isaiah 9:2-7
Theme: The Prequel

Call To Worship (Luke 2:10-12)

Do not be afraid; for see — I am bringing you good news of great joy for all the people: to you is born this day in the city of David a Savior, who is the Messiah, the Lord. This will be a sign for you: you will find a child wrapped in bands of cloth and lying in a manger.

Collect

In your light we see light. Out of the darkness we have come forward. We have seen your light. Now our light will shine before all people! Let it be so, Lord! Amen.

Prayer Of Confession (Psalm 96:10-13)

One: Say among the nations, "The Lord is king! The world is firmly established; it shall never be moved. He will judge the peoples with equity."

All: Let the heavens be glad, and let the earth rejoice; let the sea roar, and all that fills it;

One: let the field exult, and everything in it. Then shall all the trees of the forest sing for joy

All: before the Lord; for he is coming, for he is coming to judge the earth. He will judge the world with righteousness, and the peoples with his truth.

Hymns

Lo, How A Rose E'er Blooming
Hark! The Herald Angels Sing
O Little Town Of Bethlehem

Christmas Eve

Second Lesson: Titus 2:11-14
Theme: It Will Happen Again

Call To Worship (adapted from Romans 16:25-27)

God is able to strengthen us according to the gospel and the proclamation of Jesus Christ. This revelation of the mystery was kept secret for long ages but is now disclosed, and through the prophetic writings is made known to all the nations, according to the command of the eternal God, to bring about the obedience of faith. Come, let us worship the only wise God, through Jesus Christ, to whom be the glory forever! Amen.

Collect

Still we wait, Lord, still we wait. Having once beheld the angels, having once heard the song, we wait for your coming in glory that the strain may once more begin, and this time never to end. We lift our hearts, we lift our voices, in anticipation, as we wait for you. Amen.

Prayer Of Confession

With humble hearts we approach the manger. Lord, as the child grows in our Gospel Readings to become Savior and King, open our eyes to the children around us, that we might wait with anticipation for your will to be done in their lives. Chastise us if we scold too eagerly. Unto us a child should be born, if we are ready to receive your gift of life in our midst. Amen.

Hymns

Angels We Have Heard On High
Good Christian Friends, Rejoice
Silent Night

Christmas Eve

Gospel Lesson: Luke 2:1-14 (15-20)
Theme: Once More, With Feeling

Call To Worship (based on Isaiah 9:2-7)

One: The people who walked in darkness have seen a great light; those who lived in a land of deep darkness — on them light has shined.

All: You have multiplied the nation, you have increased its joy; they rejoice before you as with joy at the harvest, as people exult when dividing plunder.

One: For a child has been born for us, a Son given to us; authority rests upon his shoulders;

All: and he is named Wonderful Counselor, Mighty God, Everlasting Father, Prince of Peace.

One: His authority shall grow continually, and there shall be endless peace for the throne of David and his kingdom.

All: He will establish and uphold it with justice and with righteousness from this time onward and forevermore. The zeal of the Lord of hosts will do this.

Collect

You, Christ, our Savior are born. You are born again in our hearts. We will bear you out into the world. Amen.

Prayer Of Confession

Father of all, what have we to offer compared to the glorious gift of your Son to our broken world? Even so, help us to call to mind those who are suffering, those who are hungry, those who are cold, those who are hurting. As we dedicate our lives to your service, we pray that you will fill our hearts with the good things of your kingdom — steadfast love, compassionate mercy, and the peace that passes all understanding. Amen.

Hymns

The First Noel
Joy To The World
The Virgin Mary Had A Baby Boy

Christmas Day

First Lesson: Isaiah 62:6-12
Theme: Looking Back To Look Forward

Call To Worship (based on Isaiah 62:11-12)

See, your salvation comes; his reward is with him, and his recompense before him. You shall now be called "The Holy People, The Redeemed of the Lord."

Collect

With the coming of your Son, we see at last our salvation and our reward. Dwell with us, Lord Jesus, now and forever. Amen.

Prayer Of Confession (based on Isaiah 62:10)

Rise up, we who are the people of God. Let us go through, go through the gates, prepare the way for the people, build up, build up the highway, clear it of stones, lift up an ensign over the peoples. Let us show by our actions and our prayers that we are the long-awaited people of God. Amen.

Hymns

Away In A Manger (regular tune)
The First Noel
It Came Upon A Midnight Clear

Christmas Day

Second Lesson: Titus 3:4-7
Theme: The Hope Of Eternal Life

Call To Worship (Psalm 98)

One: O sing to the Lord a new song, for he has done marvelous things. His right hand and his holy arm have gotten him victory.

All: The Lord has made known his victory; he has revealed his vindication in the sight of the nations.

One: He has remembered his steadfast love and faithfulness to the house of Israel. All the ends of the earth have seen the victory of our God.

All: Make a joyful noise to the Lord, all the earth; break forth into joyous song and sing praises.

One: Sing praises to the Lord with the lyre, with the lyre and the sound of melody.

All: With trumpets and the sound of the horn make a joyful noise before the king, the Lord.

One: Let the sea roar, and all that fills it; the world and those who live in it.

All: Let the floods clap their hands; let the hills sing together for joy

One: at the presence of the Lord, for he is coming to judge the earth. He will judge the world with righteousness, and the peoples with equity.

Collect

Pour out your Spirit upon us this day, God of glory and might, who grants us the gift of eternal life through your Son and our Savior, Jesus Christ, the Lord. Amen.

Prayer Of Confession

This thing has been done, not by any plan of ours, not for any merit of ours, not because of any gift of ours, but because you, God of history, chose to redeem your people, chose to redeem all people, through the gift of your Son, Jesus, who is born this day. We confess with joy that we all are heirs of this eternal promise, reborn to the hope of peace. Amen.

Hymns

O Little Town Of Bethlehem
Good Christian Friends, Rejoice
What Child Is This?

Christmas Day

Gospel Lesson: Luke 2:(1-7) 8-20
Theme: The Present You Never Dreamed Of

Call To Worship

Come to the manger, ye hopeless and tired.
Shed all your cares with your greed.
Though in the wiles of worldliness mired
You may be lost — come — be freed.
God has supplied what we need.

Collect

Joy, joy, everlasting joy has once more come into our midst with your entry into the world. We praise you and thank you. Amen.

Prayer Of Confession (adapted from 1 John 1:1-4, 14)

One: We declare to you what was from the beginning, what we have heard, what we have seen with our eyes, what we have looked at and touched with our hands, concerning the Word of life —

All: this life was revealed, and we have seen it and testify to it, and declare to you the eternal life that was with the Father and was revealed to us —

One: we declare to you what we have seen and heard so that you also may have fellowship with us; and truly our fellowship is with the Father and with his Son, Jesus Christ.

All: We are proclaiming these things so that our joy may be complete — that the Word became flesh and lived among us, and we have seen his glory, the glory as of a Father's only Son, full of grace and truth.

Hymns

O Come All Ye Faithful
Silent Night
Joy To The World

First Sunday After Christmas

First Lesson: 1 Samuel 2:18-20, 26
Theme: Roots

Call To Worship (Psalm 8)

O Lord, our Sovereign, how majestic is your name in all the earth!
You have set your glory above the heavens.

Out of the mouths of babes and infants you have founded a bulwark because of your foes, to silence the enemy and the avenger.

When I look at your heavens, the work of your fingers, the moon and the stars that you have established; what are human beings that you are mindful of them, mortals that you care for them?

Yet you have made them a little lower than God, and crowned them with glory and honor.

You have given them dominion over the works of your hands; you have put all things under their feet, all sheep and oxen, and also the beasts of the field, the birds of the air, and the fish of the sea, whatever passes along the paths of the seas.

O Lord, our Sovereign, how majestic is your name in all the earth!

Collect

Lord, we are all your children, and our lives should rightfully be dedicated to you. Our every word, each action, all intentions, should be pointed toward your kingdom. We resolve with your strength to make this time yours. Amen.

Prayer Of Confession (based on Psalm 148)

Lord, at the close of this year we praise you! As we start a new year, we praise you! We are not alone in this praise. Men and women of good will around the world praise you. The angels praise you. The sun, moon, and stars praise you in the heavens. Every creature on the earth or in the heights or in the seas praises you. All growing things praise you. The winds praise you, the winter's silence praises you. Your will is perfectly performed all around us. We resolve again, with your help, to find your will for our lives as individuals and as a congregation as we gather today in praise. Let your Spirit dwell among us. Let your Son be our Savior. Lord, bless us in our gathering, and in our going forth today. Amen.

Hymns

My Soul Proclaims With Wonder
To Us A Child Of Hope Is Born
Let Our Gladness Have No End

First Sunday After Christmas

Second Lesson: Colossians 3:12-17
Theme: Grow In Favor With The Lord!

Call To Worship (Psalm 148)

Praise the Lord! Praise the Lord from the heavens; praise him in the heights!

Praise him, all his angels; praise him, all his host!

Praise him, sun and moon; praise him, all you shining stars!

Praise him, you highest heavens, and you waters above the heavens!

Let them praise the name of the Lord, for he commanded and they were created.

He established them forever and ever; he fixed their bounds, which cannot be passed.

Praise the Lord from the earth, you sea monsters and all deeps, fire and hail, snow and frost, stormy wind fulfilling his command!

Mountains and all hills, fruit trees and all cedars!

Wild animals and all cattle, creeping things and flying birds!

Kings of the earth and all peoples, princes and all rulers of the earth!

Young men and women alike, old and young together!

Let them praise the name of the Lord, for his name alone is exalted; his glory is above earth and heaven.

He has raised up a horn for his people, praise for all his faithful, for the people of Israel who are close to him. Praise the Lord!

Collect (based on Colossians 3:17)

Whatever we do, in word or deed, let us do everything in the name of the Lord Jesus, giving thanks to God the Father through him.

Prayer Of Confession

God of compassion, of steadfast love and care, please call to mind our concerns and joys. Strengthen us for what we must endure. We know you share our burdens, even when your presence is unfelt. We praise you in the midst of difficulties, and ask, as you hear our prayers, that we may continue to rely on you throughout our lives. Amen.

Hymns

Infant Holy, Infant Lowly
Where Charity And Love Prevail
Forgive Our Sins As We Forgive

First Sunday After Christmas

Gospel Lesson: Luke 2:41-52
Theme: Talk To Me, Not Through Me

Call To Worship (based on Isaiah 43:19)

God is about to do a new thing; now it springs forth, do you not perceive it?

Collect

Lord, you have called us a name — your children. We seek to live up to your trust in us, not just as individuals, but as your people called together in our sins to be perfected by you. We give thanks, we rejoice in your goodness. Bless us in our worship today. Amen.

Prayer Of Confession

Frustrated and frightened as you made her, Lord Jesus, yet your mother set us an example. She did not lash out and call you a name. She named her own feelings and how your actions had affected her. May we do likewise, naming our feelings but not scorning and naming others by our perceptions.

Hymns

Good Christian Friends, Rejoice
Away In A Manger (regular tune)
Hark! The Herald Angels Sing

Second Sunday After Christmas

First Lesson: Jeremiah 31:7-14
Theme: Turnaround Is Fair Play

Call To Worship

Let us gather together in praise, turning away from the lures of the world and returning again to the God who found us when we scarcely realized we were lost and saved us when we preferred sinking into the world's distractions.

Collect

Lord, we rejoice in your comfort and mercy. Move among us today, shaking our hearts and opening our eyes. Amen.

Prayer Of Confession

Lord, we should come back to you weeping, lamenting with tears our many sins and rejoicing with tears over the bounty of your salvation. Yet, we tend to come into your presence smug and self-satisfied, certain that we are somehow your chosen people, content to let the clock run out of time while there is so much ministry still to be shared. Convict us, cure us, cleanse us, Lord, as we depart, claiming your service. Turn our mourning into joy only when we have returned to you. Amen.

Hymns

Be Thou Our Vision
Great Is Thy Faithfulness
You Shall Go Out With Joy

Second Sunday After Christmas

Second Lesson: Ephesians 1:3-14
Theme: The Reading Of The Will

Call To Worship

Children, daughters and sons of God, let us gather in recognition that our inheritance is glorious, our task gratifying, our destiny assured.

Collect

Praise God, who not content in merely saving us, has chosen to include all humanity as family sharing one calling, all named by Jesus. Amen.

Prayer Of Confession

In every person, Lord, we read
Your word writ large and small.
May we address each human need
Acknowledging your call.
Amen.

Hymns

Children Of The Heavenly Father
Immortal Invisible
Revive Us Again

Second Sunday After Christmas

Gospel Lesson: John 1:(1-9) 10-18
Theme: True Confession

Call To Worship (Isaiah 52:7-10)

One: How beautiful upon the mountains are the feet of the messenger who announces peace, who brings good news, who announces salvation, who says to Zion, "Your God reigns."

All: Listen! Your sentinels lift up their voices, together they sing for joy; for in plain sight they see the return of the Lord to Zion.

One: Break forth together into singing, you ruins of Jerusalem; for the Lord has comforted his people, he has redeemed Jerusalem.

All: The Lord has bared his holy arm before the eyes of all the nations; and all the ends of the earth shall see the salvation of our God.

Collect

Lord, how beautiful are the hills and mountains which you have blessed us with. How magnificent the signs of the season. How strong the wind blows! How deep the cold bites! We awake, Lord, in the midst of this power to your presence. Move in our midst, Lord. Make us your people. Bless us in our worship. Amen.

Prayer Of Confession (John 1:1-14)

(Unison) In the beginning was the Word, and the Word was with God, and the Word was God. He was in the beginning with God. All things came into being through him, and without him not one thing came into being. What has come into being in him was life, and the life was the light of all people. The light shines in the darkness, and the darkness did not overcome it.

There was a man sent from God, whose name was John. He came as a witness to testify to the light, so that all might believe through him. He himself was not the light, but he came to testify to the light. The true light, which enlightens everyone, was coming into the world. He was in the world, and the world came into being through him; yet the world did not know him. He came to what was his own, and his own people did not accept him. But to all who received him, who believed in his name, he gave power to become children of God, who were born, not of blood or of the will of the flesh or of the will of man, but of God.

And the Word became flesh and lived among us, and we have seen his glory, the glory as of a Father's only Son, full of grace and truth.

Hymns

Move In Our Midst *(see page 280)*
This Little Light Of Mine
This Is My Father's World

The Epiphany Of Our Lord

First Lesson: Isaiah 60:1-6
Theme: Witness To The Light

Call To Worship (Matthew 2:2)

(Unison) Where is the child who has been born king of the Jews? For we observed his star at its rising and have come to pay him homage.

Collect

Let your light so shine, Lord of history and time, that all nations may come together to praise your name. Amen.

Prayer Of Confession

Lord, we lift up our eyes to you. As the darkness is dispelled call us to minister to your people who come from all corners of the world to celebrate your glory. Amen.

Hymns

Morning Star, O Cheering Sight
Worship The Lord In The Beauty Of Holiness
Bright And Glorious Is The Sky

The Epiphany Of Our Lord

Second Lesson: Ephesians 3:1-12
Theme: Mystery Solved

Call To Worship

The mystery, long hidden, has been revealed as the nations come forward to seek the king. Come forward as well, God's people, and share in the glory of God's plan.

Collect (based on Psalm 72:12-13)

Lord God, you deliver the needy when they call, the poor, and those who have no helper. You have pity on the weak and the downtrodden, you save the lives of the suffering. Deliver us as well, that we might go forth and share your gospel throughout your dominion, which has no end. Amen.

Prayer Of Confession

Your new light shines among us, God. Magnify your light through our lives as we seek to share your glorious plan with all people. Amen.

Hymns

Here In This Place
When Christ's Appearing Was Made Known
How Brightly Beams The Morning

The Epiphany Of Our Lord

Gospel Lesson: Matthew 2:1-12
Theme: Stopping For Directions

Call To Worship

Gather together in God's name, you who are wise enough to still seek the infant king.

Collect

Grant righteousness and peace to we who are your heirs. Grant that we might find what we earnestly seek — a share in your kingdom, shared equally with people all over the earth. Amen.

Prayer Of Confession

Let the star of wonder still shine in our hearts as we bring you our gifts and celebrate your love. Amen.

Hymns

We Three Kings
As With Gladness Men Of Old
Lift Every Voice And Sing

First Sunday After The Epiphany/The Baptism Of Our Lord

First Lesson: Isaiah 43:1-7
Theme: For I Am With You

Call To Worship (Psalm 29)

Ascribe to the Lord, O heavenly beings, ascribe to the Lord glory and strength.

Ascribe to the Lord the glory of his name; worship the Lord in holy splendor.

The voice of the Lord is over the waters; the God of glory thunders, the Lord, over mighty waters.

The voice of the Lord is powerful; the voice of the Lord is full of majesty.

The voice of the Lord breaks the cedars; the Lord breaks the cedars of Lebanon.

He makes Lebanon skip like a calf, and Sirion like a young wild ox.

The voice of the Lord flashes forth flames of fire.

The voice of the Lord shakes the wilderness; the Lord shakes the wilderness of Kadesh.

The voice of the Lord causes the oaks to whirl, and strips the forest bare; and in his temple all say, "Glory!"

The Lord sits enthroned over the flood; the Lord sits enthroned as king forever.

May the Lord give strength to his people! May the Lord bless his people with peace!

Collect

Give strength to your people, Lord, who are the source of glory and power. We will not put our trust in princes, but in your wisdom and goodness. There is nowhere we go but you are present, no danger we face but you are with us, no puzzle we seek to untangle, but you are at our side. Thank you, Lord God Almighty. Thank you. Amen.

Prayer Of Confession (based on Isaiah 43:2)

One: When you pass through the waters,
All: God will be with us;
One: and through the rivers,
All: they shall not overwhelm us;
One: when you walk through fire
All: we shall not be burned,
One: and the flame
All: shall not consume us.

Hymns

O Worship The Lord
For Christ And The Church
What A Friend We Have In Jesus

First Sunday After The Epiphany/The Baptism Of Our Lord

Second Lesson: Acts 8:14-17
Theme: The Spirit Even Here!

Call To Worship

Blow, Wind, Weave, Spirit. Turn us inside out. Toss us upside down. Surely the Lord is in this place. Do we know it?

Collect

Lord, we are so confident that we sometimes assume the presence of your Spirit. Instead of demanding, we humbly beg that hands will be laid upon us as we accept your breath in our lives. Amen.

Prayer Of Confession (to be used with a service of anointing)

Leader: I anoint you with oil for the forgiveness of your sins, the healing of your body, and the restoration of wholeness in your soul.

Hymns

Lord, I Want To Be A Christian
Wade In The Water
Jesus Calls Us

First Sunday After The Epiphany/The Baptism Of Our Lord

Gospel Lesson: Luke 3:15-17, 21-22
Theme: God Remains Pleased With Us

Call To Worship

God calls us by name and remains well pleased! Come, God's people, and adore.

Collect

Lord, your power and glory are revealed in all things great and small. Shine brighter, Lord. Shout louder, Lord. Breathe most powerfully through our lives so that the whole world acknowledges your power. Burst into history and change things for us, or burst into our hearts and help us to change this world of yours. You have given us a new year, Lord. Give us new hearts. Amen.

Prayer Of Confession

Lord, from the depths of our souls we cry to you. Our pain is known to you. Our joy is known to you. Abide with us through both. Send your healing Spirit where it is needed. Hear our prayers today. Amen.

Hymns

I Am Thine, O Lord
On Jordan's Banks The Baptist's Cry
Come Gracious Spirit

Second Sunday After The Epiphany

First Lesson: Isaiah 62:1-5
Theme: An Arranged Marriage

Call To Worship (based on Isaiah 62:1)

For Zion's sake let us not keep silent, and for Jerusalem's sake let us not rest, until her vindication shines out like the dawn, and her salvation like a burning torch.

Collect

There will come a time, Lord Jesus, when at your name every knee will bow. We bow our knees today, and proclaim before a lost world that you mean to find us. Our vindication is near. Amen.

Prayer Of Confession

Lord Jesus, we are your bride, yet we shy away from your images which call us to a closer relationship. We fear intimacy and draw back, seeking to protect some bit of our fallen nature, something we mistake for our identity, but which is a falling away from you. Come and claim us, Lord. Amen.

Hymns

Come, Now Is The Time To Worship
Rock Of Ages
What Wondrous Love Is This?

Second Sunday After The Epiphany

Second Lesson: 1 Corinthians 12:1-11
Theme: I See It Now

Call To Worship (adapted from Psalm 36:9)

With God is the fountain of life. In God's light we see light.

Collect

Lord in heaven, we come to you as a people of many gifts. We come to you as the people of one Spirit, one God. The world seeks to divide us into 1,000 identities, but in our diversity we see clearly that you call us to be one body in Christ. We come today to offer our gifts to you that we might grow in service and wisdom. Send your Spirit to dwell with us today. Amen.

Prayer Of Confession

So many gifts, Lord, you have scattered among us. Rather than scramble to claim another's gift we praise you today for the blessings you have provided each one of us, treasures we are to share, not hoard. Thank you, Lord, for the diversity of your fellowship. May it be that all humanity, all cultures, all races, all ages, all economies, all nations, friend and enemy, may be gathered in your name to create at last your kingdom. Amen.

Hymns

They'll Know We Are Christians By Our Love
There Are Many Gifts, But The Same Spirit
God Be With You Till We Meet Again

Second Sunday After The Epiphany

Gospel Lesson: John 2:1-11
Theme: Mother Knows Best

Call To Worship (Psalm 36:5-10)

One: Your steadfast love, O Lord, extends to the heavens, your faithfulness to the clouds.

All: Your righteousness is like the mighty mountains, your judgments are like the great deep; you save humans and animals alike, O Lord.

Right Side: How precious is your steadfast love, O God! All people may take refuge in the shadow of your wings.

Left Side: They feast on the abundance of your house, and you give them drink from the river of your delights.

Younger: For with you is the fountain of life; in your light we see light.

Older: O continue your steadfast love to those who know you, and your salvation to the upright of heart!

Collect

Though the feast was in danger, yet you multiplied joy. May we in celebration continue to raise our happy voices, casting aside a false solemnity and embracing your salvation. Amen.

Prayer Of Confession

We thank you, Jesus, for filling a need though you claimed it was not yet your time. No matter what time we are called to serve, may we follow your example whether or not we feel ready, think it is time, or have confidence at all in our abilities. In your strength we will serve. Amen.

Hymns

Sweet Are The Promises
Like The Murmur Of The Dove's Song
Trust And Obey

Third Sunday After The Epiphany

First Lesson: Nehemiah 8:1-3, 5-6, 8-10
Theme: The Meaning, With Interpretations

Call To Worship (based on Psalm 19)

One: The heavens are telling the glory of God; and the firmament proclaims his handiwork.

All: Day to day pours forth speech, and night to night declares knowledge.

One: There is no speech, nor are there words; their voice is not heard;

All: yet their voice goes out through all the earth, and their words to the end of the world.

One: The law of the Lord is perfect, reviving the soul; the decrees of the Lord are sure, making wise the simple;

All: the precepts of the Lord are right, rejoicing the heart; the commandment of the Lord is clear, enlightening the eyes;

One: the fear of the Lord is pure, enduring forever; the ordinances of the Lord are true and righteous altogether.

All: Let the words of my mouth and the meditation of my heart be acceptable to you, O Lord, my rock and my redeemer.

Collect

With a pleasure that is equal parts tears and laughter we come before your presence, ready to hear your Word, with interpretations, that as your people we might grow in love and fellowship. Amen.

Prayer Of Confession

Not by ourselves, but together, with the aid of your Spirit, may we find the key to unlock your scriptures. Not arrogantly assuming we only are the source of wisdom, but together, as many churches, do we seek your light. Not as one nation, but as believers spread among all nations, may we come to understand at last your will for our lives. Teach us to listen as well as speak with each other. Amen.

Hymns

Thy Word
Glorious Things Of Thee Are Spoken
Lamp Of Our Feet

Third Sunday After The Epiphany

Second Lesson: 1 Corinthians 12:12-31a
Theme: Eye, Ear, Nose, And Throat

Call To Worship (based on 1 Corinthians 12:27, 31)

Now you are the body of Christ and individually members of it. Strive for the greater gifts.

Collect

Lord of the heavens, the skies tell us the story of your work. Day to day pours forth speech, and night to night declares knowledge. They speak no words, but your Word is writ large in creation all around us. Help us to read that Word, not only for our benefit, but also for the blessing of all nations and all people. Your sun, your moon, your rain, your winds, are for all people. You desire to draw us together. Call us through our worship today to be proclaimers of your Word. Amen.

Prayer Of Confession

Lord, to you all things are known. From you nothing is hidden. You know, from our words and from our silence, what is the wish of our hearts. Grant our petitions this morning. Hear our earnest prayers. Amen.

Hymns

Holy, Holy, Holy
Bind Us Together In Love
There Are Many Gifts, But The Same Spirit

Third Sunday After The Epiphany

Gospel Lesson: Luke 4:14-21
Theme: True Is True

Call To Worship (Psalm 19:7, 10)

The law of the Lord is perfect, reviving the soul; the decrees of the Lord are sure, making wise the simple. More to be desired are they than gold, even much fine gold; sweeter also than honey, and drippings of the honeycomb.

Collect

Lord, we long to hear your Word spoken aloud by a reader, spoken again by your Spirit directly in our hearts. Amen.

Prayer Of Confession

May we hear your words, blessed by your grace and patience, receiving your commission, restored in your love. Amen.

Hymns

Hail To The Lord's Anointed!
We Give Thee But Thine Own
Wonderful Grace Of Jesus

Fourth Sunday After The Epiphany

First Lesson: Jeremiah 1:4-10
Theme: The Call Is For You

Call To Worship (based on Psalm 71:3)

God is our a rock of refuge, a strong fortress. Save us, God, for you are our rock and our fortress.

Collect

Gracious Lord, our rock and our refuge, in you we place our hope and trust. Call us to be your faithful people this morning. Inspire us through the presence of your Holy Spirit to accept the tasks you have given us, and to joyfully fulfill your will in our world. Amen.

Prayer Of Confession

Only — Lord we often excuse ourselves by saying we are only a youth, only one person, only too busy, only not ready, only one church. But you have been waiting for us since before birth, and you are more than only God. We accept your call and answer it willingly this day. Amen.

Hymns

In The Rifted Rock I'm Resting
Here I Am, Lord
Come Thou Font Of Many Blessings

Fourth Sunday After The Epiphany

Second Lesson: 1 Corinthians 13:1-13
Theme: The Antidote

Call To Worship (based on Psalm 138:6-8)

Lord we know that though you are high above all creation, you regard the lowly. Though we walk through the midst of trouble, you preserve us. You stretch out your hand and deliver us. Lord, fulfill your purpose for us. Your steadfast love, O Lord, endures forever. Do not forsake the work of your hands, but answer our prayers, hear our joys and concerns, unspoken and spoken. Draw us together as your people. Amen.

Collect

Lord, you are our rock of refuge. The storms of life swirl around us. We need an anchor in that storm. You have heard our joys and concerns, spoken and unspoken. We pray you have also heard the faithfulness in our petition, for in asking you for aid we proclaim your power and admit our need. Bless us as your people. Heal us. Amen.

Prayer Of Confession

True love. What is true love? True love is the love of a scarred back torn by splinters, the love of a forehead pierced by thorns, the love of hands and feet cut by nails, the love of a body scored by wounds. True love creates summer breezes and howling winter winds, true love calls the corn from the soil, and is a love whose very *no* means *yes* to life for many. We have seen this love in action in our own lives. Let us live it.

Hymns

The Old Rugged Cross
May The Grace Of Christ Our Savior
Though I May Give (O Waly Waly)

Fourth Sunday After The Epiphany

Gospel Lesson: Luke 4:21-30
Theme: Jesus Speaks Now

Call To Worship

One: Lord, we gather together this morning.

All: We are your people, Lord. You have made us what we are.

Right Side: We are young.

Left Side: We are not as young as we were!

Men: We are rich by the standards of the world.

Women: We do not feel as rich as we are.

Upstairs: We are many, ready to work for the kingdom.

Downstairs: But we feel like so few when we consider the work to be done.

One: You are our Lord, who we gather to worship today.

All: We are yours. Breathe on us, breath of God. Remold us today in your image and your will.

Collect

Lord, sometimes it seems like everyone is living the life of the risen Lord, and we're only now starting to get it. By the grace of God we are what we are, and we know your grace toward us has not been in vain. Call us to work harder than ever for your kingdom. Speak to us in the words and the silences and the songs as we answer your insistent call, saying, "Here we are, Lord. Send us!" Amen.

Prayer Of Confession

How long the neighbors had waited to hear Jesus, but his words challenged them and they rejected him. Don't we call for your return as well, yet we reject the notion that your Word is fulfilled in our midst and refuse to hear the messengers you have placed among us to challenge us to proclaim the year of the Lord's favor? May we yet, with your help, share the good news with the poor, the outcast, the ailing, that we might all be saved. Amen.

Hymns

When I Survey The Wondrous Cross
God, Make Us Your Family
Just As I Am

Fifth Sunday After The Epiphany

First Lesson: Isaiah 6:1-8 (9-13)
Theme: There Must Be Some Mistake

Call To Worship (based on Jeremiah 1:6-7, The Message)

One: But I said, "Hold it, master God! Look at me. I don't know anything. I'm only a child."

All: God told me, "Don't say, 'I'm only a child.' I'll tell you where to go and you'll go there. I'll tell you what to say and you'll say it."

Collect

Heavenly Father, we praise your name, and ask you for a full measure of your prophetic spirit as we accept your calling to go forth into the world. Though we are quick to make excuses, make us quicker to take up the mantle of evangelism, to reach out to people in our neighborhood and beyond our company to the nation at large and the four corners of the world. With faith and your strength, all things are possible. It can begin here in this place. We pray these things in your name. Amen.

Prayer Of Confession (based on Matthew 28:18-20)

Lord, God, send all of us. In your name, with your authority, we seek to make disciples among all the nations. Call us together to learn all you have commanded. We remember, Lord Jesus, you will be with us always, to the end of the age. Here we are. Send us!

Hymns

Here In This Place
Amazing Grace
Here I Am, Lord

Fifth Sunday After The Epiphany

Second Lesson: 1 Corinthians 15:1-11
Theme: I Will Explain It Slowly

Call To Worship

For believers, every Sunday is Easter Sunday, regardless of the season, regardless of the date! Come together, believers, and believe!

Collect

Risen Lord we praise your name, confident that in you all of creation will be raised! Amen.

Prayer Of Confession (based on 1 Corinthians 15:1-4)

This is the good news which has been proclaimed unto us, which we have received, and in which we stand, through which also we are being saved. We will hold firmly to the message that was proclaimed to us because we have not believed in vain. Christ died for our sins in accordance with the scriptures, he was buried, and was raised on the third day according to the scriptures!

Hymns

Christ The Lord Is Risen Today
Up From The Grave He Arose
Because He Lives

Fifth Sunday After The Epiphany

Gospel Lesson: Luke 5:1-11
Theme: Big Fish, Big Pond

Call To Worship (Psalm 138:1-2)

I give you thanks, O Lord, with my whole heart; before the gods I sing your praise; I bow down toward your holy temple and give thanks to your name for your steadfast love and your faithfulness; for you have exalted your name and your word above everything.

Collect

Lord, this morning we reach out to our community and to the world through our offerings. We strive to be your faithful people, and with your help we shall succeed. Reveal your will to us through this time of worship. Amen.

Prayer Of Confession

The grace of God is with us! Let us share together the sign of God's peace as we confess that we are saved through his holy name. Amen.

Hymns

Two Fishermen
I Know Whom I Have Believed
Forward Through The Ages

Sixth Sunday After The Epiphany

First Lesson: Jeremiah 17:5-10
Theme: Heavenly Horticulture

Call To Worship (Psalm 1)

Happy are those who do not follow the advice of the wicked, or take the path that sinners tread, or sit in the seat of scoffers; but their delight is in the law of the Lord, and on his law they meditate day and night.

They are like trees planted by streams of water, which yield their fruit in its season, and their leaves do not wither. In all that they do, they prosper.

The wicked are not so, but are like chaff that the wind drives away.

Therefore the wicked will not stand in the judgment, nor sinners in the congregation of the righteous; for the Lord watches over the way of the righteous, but the way of the wicked will perish.

Collect

Lord, today we choose your way, ready to stand against the fading fashions of our day, true to our calling, confident in your Word. Amen.

Prayer Of Confession

Our delight is in the law of the Lord! Let us put down deep roots in the waters that flow from God's Word into our daily lives. Amen.

Hymns

Thy Word
How Bless'd Are They Who, Fearing God
Open My Eyes That I May See

Sixth Sunday After The Epiphany

Second Lesson: 1 Corinthians 15:12-20
Theme: Least To Be Pitied, More To Be Emulated

Call To Worship (1 Corinthians 15:19-20)

One: If for this life only we have hoped in Christ, we are of all people most to be pitied.

All: But in fact Christ has been raised from the dead, the first fruits of those who have died.

Collect

Accept, O Lord, our hearts today. We trust that you will guide us in the work of your kingdom. With a cheerful heart we give to you. With hope we receive from you. Bless us all in this time of worship. Amen.

Prayer Of Confession

Lord, we speak from the heart about our concerns and joys. We speak because we know you are listening. We speak because we know our sisters and brothers are listening as well. Inspire us to help where we are needed, and to wait for your guidance in our times of celebration and sorrow. Stand by us through all the experiences of our lives. Amen.

Hymns

This Joyful Eastertide
Christ Is Risen! Shout Hosanna
I Serve A Risen Savior

Sixth Sunday After The Epiphany

Gospel Lesson: Luke 6:17-26
Theme: Joys And Woes

Call To Worship

One: Jesus turns everything upside down.
All: The kingdom of God is topsy-turvy.
Women: Jesus said, "Blessed are you who are poor, for yours is the kingdom of God."
Men: Jesus said, "But woe to you who are rich, for you have received our consolation."
Left Side: Jesus said, "Blessed are you who are hungry now, for you will be filled."
Right Side: Jesus said, "Woe to you who are full now, for you will be hungry."
Younger: Jesus said, "Blessed are you who weep now, for you will laugh."
Older: Jesus said, "Woe to you who are laughing now, for you will mourn and weep."
One: Jesus told us, "Rejoice in that day and leap for joy, for surely your reward is great in heaven."
All: Let us pray!

Collect

Lord Jesus, we will rejoice, and we rejoice now that we exhibit the marks of the kingdom. We are hungry for peace. We are poor compared to the faithfulness of our brothers and sisters around the undeveloped world. We weep as we consider what we have left undone in your kingdom. Fill our hungry, cure our poverty, set us laughing. Hear our earnest prayer as we come to worship you this day. Our lives are filled with woes. Turn our woe to rejoicing. These things we pray in your name. Amen.

Prayer Of Confession

Let us rejoice and leap for joy, regardless of what the world thinks, for our reward is great in heaven!

Hymns

Come, Let Us All Unite To Sing
Dona Nobis Pacem
Who Now Would Follow Christ?

Seventh Sunday After The Epiphany

First Lesson: Genesis 45:3-11, 15
Theme: Slow Burn

Call To Worship

Regardless of our ill intentions, God means all things for God, and will, despite our best efforts to derail his kingdom, see his will done on earth as it is heaven! Rejoice!

Collect

Lord, we accept the forgiveness you offer. Though we have carefully measured out what we will forgive and what we won't forget, we pray that thanks to your lavish measure of grace we will be freed to receive your unabated blessings together, in the presence of friends and now former enemies. Amen.

Prayer Of Confession

Lord, I offer up to you this day the ill will I harbor toward others, the finely aged grudge, the misplaced sense of injustice. Grant us in return your heavenly justice, which is found in reconciliation and peace. Amen.

Hymns

Trust And Obey
Surely The Presence
Nearer My God To Thee

Seventh Sunday After The Epiphany

Second Lesson: 1 Corinthians 15:35-38, 42-50
Theme: Hard To Get Parts For The Older Models

Call To Worship (based on Psalm 37)

One: Trust in the Lord, and do good.
All: Take delight in the Lord, and he will give you the desires of your heart.
Right Side: Commit your way to the Lord; trust in God to act.
Left Side: God will make your vindication shine like the light, and the justice of your cause like the noonday.
Women: Be still before the Lord, and wait patiently.
All: The meek shall inherit the land, and delight themselves in abundant prosperity.

Collect

Lead us in your paths of righteousness, not just for your name's sake, but for our sake as well! Amen.

Prayer Of Confession

It is dangerous, Lord, to pour new wine into old wineskins. Lest we burst we pray that you will renew and restore our hope in the risen Christ, that we might begin to live by the hope of your kingdom. Amen.

Hymns

There Is A Place Of Quiet Rest
All Hail The Power Of Jesus' Name (Coronation)
To God Be The Glory

Seventh Sunday After The Epiphany

Gospel Lesson: Luke 6:27-38
Theme: Yes, Love THAT Enemy, Too!

Call To Worship

Love your enemy. Yes, that enemy. Do good to those who hate you. Really hate you. Our reward is great, and the reward might be even greater for those who wish us harm, even salvation shared in Christ Jesus.

Collect

God of justice, we wait for the coming of your kingdom, and pray that your kingdom comes soon. Inspire us to live by your rules in the light of the Word. In our gathering today share your Spirit as we seek you in prayer and praise. Open our hearts to your inspiration. These things we pray in the name of the risen Christ. Amen.

Prayer Of Confession

This day we come to you with our joys and concerns, as we have done many times before. We have seen our prayers answered. The answer has been, "Yes." The answer has been, "No." The answer has been mysterious. The answer has been surprising. You have kept faith with us. We return, and keep faith with you. One thing has remained constant — we know you have heard us. Great is your faithfulness, Lord. Great are you, Lord. We ask that once again you hear us, and in your time, respond to us. Hear our praise. Hear our pleas. Amen.

Hymns

Great Is The Lord
O Perfect Love, All Human Thought Transcending
Great Is Thy Faithfulness

Eighth Sunday After The Epiphany

First Lesson: Isaiah 55:10-13
Theme: Full Circle, Full Cycle

Call To Worship (based on Deuteronomy 32:2)

May God's teaching drop like the rain, God's speech condense like the dew; like gentle rain on grass, like showers on new growth.

Collect

Plant your seed within our hearts, gardening God, that we might bear fruit worthy of your kingdom. Amen.

Prayer Of Confession

We repent from dust and ashes, Lord, accepting your forgiveness, and intent that we shall live forgiven, and go out with joy! Amen.

Hymns

O Let All Who Thirst
In The Bulb There Is A Flower
You Shall Go Out With Joy

Eighth Sunday After The Epiphany

Second Lesson: 1 Corinthians 15:51-58
Theme: Mystery Solved

Call To Worship (Isaiah 25:6-9)

One: On this mountain the Lord of hosts will make for all peoples a feast of rich food, a feast of well-aged wines, of rich food filled with marrow, of well-aged wines strained clear.

All: And he will destroy on this mountain the shroud that is cast over all peoples, the sheet that is spread over all nations; he will swallow up death forever.

One: Then the Lord God will wipe away the tears from all faces, and the disgrace of his people he will take away from all the earth, for the Lord has spoken.

All: It will be said on that day, Lo, this is our God; we have waited for him, so that he might save us. This is the Lord for whom we have waited; let us be glad and rejoice in his salvation.

Collect

Let your trumpet resound, annoying us enough that we might drop our worldly cares to embrace the hope we have in you. Amen.

Prayer Of Confession

Lord, even as we pray we expect your return. Even as we pray we feel your call to service. Whatever your will might be for today, may we be found at our post, faithful to your kingdom, your willing servants ever. Amen.

Hymns

Open My Eyes That I May See
Guide My Feet
Soon And Very Soon

Eighth Sunday After The Epiphany

Gospel Lesson: Luke 6:39-49
Theme: Demote The Mote

Call To Worship

God knows these children who are gathered today. It is all of us, with all our faults. Let us thank God for all blessings. Let us see each other clearly. Let us cherish all of creation.

Collect

Lord, we cast aside illusions as we approach ever closer the season of Lent. We confront our own shortcomings and celebrate your grace. *Marana Tha*. Come, Lord Jesus. Amen.

Prayer Of Confession

(Rest in silence. Let one read Luke 6:46 aloud)
Why do you call me "Lord, Lord," and do not do what I tell you?
(Rest in silence. Let one read Luke 6:46 aloud again)
Why do you call me "Lord, Lord," and do not do what I tell you?
(Rest in silence. Let one read Luke 6:46 a final time)
Why do you call me "Lord, Lord," and do not do what I tell you?
(Rest in silence.)
Amen.

Hymns

Lord, Listen To Your Children Praying
Lift Every Voice And Sing
For All The Saints

The Transfiguration Of Our Lord
(Last Sunday After The Epiphany)

First Lesson: Exodus 34:29-35
Theme: Too Bright

Call To Worship

Come forward, people of God. What others might find too bright we endure and enjoy in the hope that when all else is burned away, we shall be revealed as God's gold.

Collect

Great God of glory, we thank you for your Word. May it shine as brightly in our hearts as your glory was reflected off the countenance of Moses, that all in darkness might come to know you. Amen.

Prayer Of Confession

Humbly we come before you, Lord of mercy, aware of our shortcomings, but saved by our hope in you. Amen.

Hymns

In The Rifted Rock I'm Resting
Immortal Invisible
Are Ye Able?

The Transfiguration Of Our Lord
(Last Sunday After The Epiphany)

Second Lesson: 2 Corinthians 3:12—4:2
Theme: Ready?

Call To Worship (based on 2 Corinthians 3:18)

Let us all, with unveiled faces, behold the glory of the Lord as though reflected in a mirror, that we might be transformed into the same image from one degree of glory to another; for this comes from the Lord, the Spirit.

Collect (based on the *Didache*)

As the wheat is harvested from every hill to be baked in one golden loaf, so we pray that you will call us from every nation, every race, with every gift, women and men, ground together in your love, that we might be presented as a single, perfect sacrifice. Amen.

Prayer Of Confession

Remove the veil we have draped over our hearts, that we might fully bear each other's burdens in your name. Amen.

Hymns

Awake, Awake, To Love And Work
Love Divine, All Loves Excelling
Lo, A Gleam From Yonder Heaven

The Transfiguration Of Our Lord
(Last Sunday After The Epiphany)

Gospel Lesson: Luke 9:28-36 (37-43)
Theme: Is That Really You?

Call To Worship (based on Psalm 99)

One: The Lord is king; let the peoples tremble!
All: He sits enthroned upon the cherubim; let the earth quake!
One: The Lord is great in Zion; he is exalted over all the peoples.
All: Let them praise your great and awesome name. Holy is he!
One: Mighty King, lover of justice, you have established equity; you have executed justice and righteousness in Jacob.
All: Extol the Lord our God, and worship at his holy mountain; for the Lord our God is holy.

Collect

We praise you for your love for us, and for this opportunity to return even if only in part, some measure of what you have granted to your people. Accept our worship this morning as a clear sign that your kingdom is in our midst. Amen.

Prayer Of Confession

Lord, your Holy Spirit speaks to us, not in cleverly devised myths, but in truth. We hear this truth not only in your Word, but in your words spoken through that Spirit in our hearts. We hear this truth in the concerns and joys of our sisters and brothers gathered here in your assembly. Open our hearts, open our minds, open our wills, that we may perfectly love you and serve you, while we love and serve your people both near and far. These things we pray in your name. Amen.

Hymns

Breathe On Me, Breath Of God
Christ Upon The Mountain Peak
In The Cross Of Christ I Glory

Ash Wednesday

First Lesson: Joel 2:1-2, 12-17
Theme: Lost And Found

Call To Worship (Psalm 51:1, 6)

One: Have mercy on me, O God, according to your steadfast love; according to your abundant mercy blot out my transgressions.

All: You desire truth in the inward being; therefore teach me wisdom in my secret heart.

Collect

We quiet our hearts and open our minds to your presence as we gather on this solemn occasion, aware both of our sins and of the opportunity for forgiveness. Amen.

Prayer Of Confession

(Worshipers come forward. As ashes are applied one worship leader says:)

Receive these ashes as a reminder of those sins that separate us from God and each other.

(The worshiper walks to the side. A small towel is dipped in water and handed to the worshiper by a second worship leader who says:)

Receive God's forgiveness, now and always, and walk in the light of God's love.

(The worshiper may wipe away the ashes.)

Hymns

Oh, Love, How Deep
The Glory Of These Forty Days
Out Of The Depths

Ash Wednesday

Second Lesson: 2 Corinthians 5:20b—6:10
Theme: Hit Me With Your Best Shot

Call To Worship

Nobody said it would be easy to follow Christ. Just good.

Collect

Comforting God, in the dark places of our lives, in the suffering, in times of alienation, we need you most. Thank you for your presence as we meditate not only upon our sins, but on your forgiveness. Amen.

Prayer Of Confession

We confess that there is no place we can go, no sin we might commit, no error we may stray into, no nook or cranny of life's circumstances we may lose our way within, that you cannot find us, Lord, nor will you ever cease to seek us and to save us. Amen.

Hymns

In Your Sickness, Your Sufferings, Your Trials And Pains
When I Survey The Wondrous Cross
A Charge To Keep

Ash Wednesday

Gospel Lesson: Matthew 6:1-6, 16-21
Theme: No Peeking

Call To Worship

Come to a special place, people of God, where in the quiet of our hearts we may seek the creator of the universe, the Lord of life, and the friend of each one of us.

Collect

We thank you, Lord, that you are not impressed with how great a show we make in public, but how great a change we make in our lives as disciples committed to the work of your kingdom. Amen.

Prayer Of Confession

(Worshipers who come forward will receive ashes upon the forehead as well as a small moist towel.)

Receive these ashes as a symbol of your sins. They are easily wiped away. You may retain the visible mark of your sins only as long as you choose, and receive God's forgiveness as easily as you may wipe this mark away. Rejoice. God is always with us, and forgiveness is always possible.

Hymns

Softly And Tenderly Jesus Is Calling
Jubilate Deo
Christian, Let Your Burning Light

First Sunday In Lent

First Lesson: Deuteronomy 26:1-11
Theme: The Father We All Share

Call To Worship (based on Psalm 92)

One: It is good to give thanks to the Lord, to sing praises to your name, O Most High;

All: to declare your steadfast love in the morning, and your faithfulness by night,

Left Side: to the music of the lute and the harp, to the melody of the lyre.

Right Side: For you, O Lord, have made me glad by your work; at the works of your hands I sing for joy.

Upstairs: How great are your works, O Lord! Your thoughts are very deep!

Downstairs: The righteous flourish like the palm tree, and grow like a cedar in Lebanon.

Men: They are planted in the house of the Lord; they flourish in the courts of our God.

Women: In old age they still produce fruit; they are always green and full of sap,

All: showing that the Lord is upright; he is my rock, and there is no unrighteousness in him.

Collect

Lord, what we call ours was always yours, every moment, every vision, every acre. We offer up to you only that which we use in your name, and pray that our offerings will glorify your work. Amen.

Prayer Of Confession

God of the tabernacle, who accompanied the people in the desert, we confess that we strive to pin you down, to hold you fast within the walls of a church, to keep ourselves safe by limiting your access to our lives. We are wanderers on this earth, and we open our hearts to your will, that we will wander, literally, spiritually, and emotionally, wherever you send us. Amen.

Hymns

Sanctuary
We Give Thee But Thine Own
As Saints Of Old

First Sunday In Lent

Second Lesson: Romans 10:8b-13
Theme: The Word Is Near You

Call To Worship (Deuteronomy 30:14, The Message)

(Unison) The Word is right here and now — as near as the tongue in your mouth, as near as the heart in your chest. Just do it!

Collect

Adults: O God, I surrender all to you.
Children: Hold me in the shadow of your wings.

Prayer Of Confession

(Unison) Everyone who calls on the Lord will be saved!

Hymns

From All That Dwell Beneath The Skies
Whosoever Heareth
You Shall Go Out With Joy!

First Sunday In Lent

Gospel Lesson: Luke 4:1-13
Theme: Satan's Best Shot

Call To Worship (based on Psalm 92)

One: It is good to give thanks to the Lord, to sing praises to your name, O Most High;

All: to declare your steadfast love in the morning, and your faithfulness by night.

Collect

Lord Jesus, our strength in our temptations is your Word and our worship. Make us glad by your Word, both in our lives and in the lives of others. Help us to take as much joy in the praise of our spiritual ancestors as we do in the wisdom expressed by our children and our seniors. Lord Jesus, you set your face upon the cross and fulfilled the scriptures. Help us to make our lives scriptures of fulfillment as well, in our worship this morning and in our lives all this week. These things we pray in your name. Amen.

Prayer Of Confession

Lord, when we stumble, be there beside us. Lord, when we doubt, be with us to uphold us. Lord, when there is need, within our congregation and in the world beyond, call us to be your presence. Hear our prayers and petitions today, and bless us in our ministry to each other and for your kingdom. Strengthen us in our weakness, instill us with courage, so that we hear the call to caring ministry. These things we pray, individually, and as the body of Christ, as we recall the words of your Son and our Savior, saying in one voice:

Our Father, who art in heaven, hallowed be thy name. Thy kingdom come. Thy will be done on earth as it is in heaven. Give us this day our daily bread, and forgive us our debts, as we forgive our debtors. And lead us not into temptation, but deliver us from evil. For thine is the kingdom, the power, and the glory, forever. Amen.

Hymns

All Creatures Of Our God And King
I Love To Tell The Story
Marvelous Grace Of Our Loving Lord

Second Sunday In Lent

First Lesson: Genesis 15:1-12, 17-18
Theme: Just In Case You Forget ...

Call To Worship

Yes, Father in heaven, we are here again, and we are here for the first time. We are your people of patience, and we wait impatiently for your kingdom. We are your light to the world, and we struggle to let that light shine. We are imperfect, but you will perfect us, in a time of your choosing. Be present with us today. Send your Spirit to dwell among us. Let your Son live in our actions. Hear us, and bless us in this time of gathering, and praising, and departing. These things we pray in your name. Amen.

Collect

Day by day, dear Lord, of thee three things I pray: to see thee more clearly, love thee more dearly, follow thee more nearly, day by day. Amen. — Richard of Chichester (c. 1197-1253)

Prayer Of Confession

We are thankful, God of long memory, that when we lose sight of your promises you will reaffirm your loving kindness and commitment. Thank you for your patience with us, your forbearance, and your love. Amen.

Hymns

We're Marching To Zion
The Lord Our God Is Clothed With Mercy
Great Is Your Faithfulness

Second Sunday In Lent

Second Lesson: Philippians 3:17—4:1
Theme: Your Belly Or Your Life

Call To Worship

Adults: O God, in a dry and desolate land I thirst. I come to the waters of your presence.

Children: O God, I seek your face.

Collect

Gracious God, we come here freely, as your Son came freely for our salvation. Accept our lives in the spirit in which they are lived. Magnify our work for your kingdom a hundredfold as we seek to do your will in this world. Amen.

Prayer Of Confession

What, Lord, can we give you that will compare to your bounty toward us? Even our prayer of thanksgiving is a prayer of your giving, for our words, our thoughts, and all that is best in us, is a gift from you. Grant our request in this time of giving that you will call us to servanthood, inspire us with vision, and magnify your generous Spirit in our actions. Amen.

Hymns

Blessed Assurance
Bread Of The World In Mercy Broken
Hark, The Voice Of Jesus Calling

Second Sunday In Lent

Gospel Lesson: Luke 13:31-35
Theme: Oh, Jerusalem

Call To Worship (based on Psalm 27)

One: God, you are my God, I seek you, my soul thirsts for you; my flesh faints for you, as in a dry and weary land where there is no water.

All: So I have looked upon you in the sanctuary, beholding your power and glory.

Women: Because your steadfast love is better than life, my lips will praise you.

Men: So I will bless you as long as I live; I will lift up my hands and call on your name.

Younger: My soul is satisfied as with a rich feast and my mouth praises you with joyful lips

Older: when I think of you on my bed, and meditate on you in the watches of the night;

Upstairs: for you have been my help, and in the shadow of your wings I sing for joy.

Downstairs: My soul clings to you; your right hand upholds me.

All: O God, you are my God, I seek you, my soul thirsts for you.

Collect

Lord, your mercy and your goodness are without price. You remember us when we feel forgotten, and seek us out when we convince ourselves to hide from you. We turn to you willingly this morning, calling upon your name, confident in your power, and hopeful in our prayers. In our worship together we will strive to be faithful. Let our witness to your glory be greater than our intent, so that at the name of Jesus every knee shall bow. Amen.

Prayer Of Confession

Lord, we know how great the needs are in the rest of the world. We know the suffering that is all around us. We lift up in our prayers today the sorrows of those we may never meet in this life, but whose situation is heavy in our hearts. We come boldly to the throne of grace with our own joys and concerns as well, confident that your love for us is as great as for your children everywhere. Hear our prayers as well as all the prayers lifted today. Hear the prayers of those who may not know how to pray. Mold us and make us into your people even as you heal us and save us. Lord, these things we pray in your mighty name. Amen.

Hymns

O Jesus Christ, My Grateful Hymns
My Faith Looks Up To Thee
O Love, How Deep

Third Sunday In Lent

First Lesson: Isaiah 55:1-9
Theme: For God Will Abundantly Pardon

Call To Worship (Isaiah 55:6-9)

One: Seek the Lord while he may be found, call upon him while he is near;

All: let the wicked forsake their way, and the unrighteous their thoughts; let them return to the Lord, that he may have mercy on them, and to our God, for he will abundantly pardon.

One: For my thoughts are not your thoughts, nor are your ways my ways, says the Lord.

All: For as the heavens are higher than the earth, so are my ways higher than your ways and my thoughts than your thoughts.

Collect

God of grace and God of glory, fill our hearts through the inspiration of your Holy Spirit with the knowledge of your great creation, and the plan you have to draw all things to you. May we see you in every sister and brother in our midst and around the world. We pray this in your mighty name. Amen.

Prayer Of Confession

Lord God of mystery and clarity, we praise your name for those blessings which are obvious to us, as well as your mercies which remain hidden from us because of our hardness of heart. As we gather together we will strive to forsake our former ways and to seek you where you may be found — in your living Word, in the praise of children, among the poor in our midst and around the world, and in your love for us. This day, this hour, we dedicate to you. We pray these things in your mighty name. Amen.

Hymns

God Of Grace And God Of Glory
Great Is The Lord
What A Friend We Have In Jesus

Third Sunday In Lent

Second Lesson: 1 Corinthians 10:1-13
Theme: There's Always A Way Out

Call To Worship (Isaiah 55:13)

Instead of the thorn shall come up the cypress; instead of the brier shall come up the myrtle; and it shall be to the Lord for a memorial, for an everlasting sign that shall not be cut off.

Collect

We see through scripture that your people can succeed or fail, follow you or lose sight of you, remember you or forget you. We come together in your name, O Lord, to follow. Amen.

Prayer Of Confession

You have told us through your Word that we cannot be tempted more than we can bear, and we thank you that to help us you have granted us not only your Holy Spirit, but our sisters and brothers. Remind us to reach out to each other in times of need, to resist depending solely on our own strength, and to find shelter in you. Amen.

Hymns

Amen, Asithi
Blessed Assurance
In The Hour Of Trial

Third Sunday In Lent

Gospel Lesson: Luke 13:1-9
Theme: Towers Fall, God Endures

Call To Worship (Psalm 63:1-8)

O God, you are my God, I seek you, my soul thirsts for you; my flesh faints for you, as in a dry and weary land where there is no water.

So I have looked upon you in the sanctuary, beholding your power and glory.

Because your steadfast love is better than life, my lips will praise you.

So I will bless you as long as I live; I will lift up my hands and call on your name.

My soul is satisfied as with a rich feast, and my mouth praises you with joyful lips when I think of you on my bed, and meditate on you in the watches of the night; for you have been my help, and in the shadow of your wings I sing for joy.

My soul clings to you; your right hand upholds me.

Collect

God of all seasons, we pray that in this time together we may look beyond bad and good fortune to your sustaining presence and present patience. Amen.

Prayer Of Confession

Chance takes a toll, and all experience pain in this life. We know, Lord, that these do not represent greater or lesser blessings, but in all things we are encouraged to seek you out, to reach out to you when disaster or sorrow strikes, and to remember you when we are anesthetized by good fortune and good health. Give us more time to mature in your Word, to become better disciples, to become better prepared for your harvest. Amen.

Hymns

Come, Come Ye Saints
Gloria
On Eagle's Wings

Fourth Sunday In Lent

First Lesson: Joshua 5:9-12
Theme: Today I Have Taken Away Your Shame

Call To Worship

Let us walk away from the security of law to the maturity of life in God's grace. Take hold of the mature discipleship God offers us as we worship together today.

Collect

Lord, you patiently wait while we decide whether we will serve you or the world. Our gifts are a part of our commitment to the gospel. Bless us in this hour of giving, and strengthen our resolve for your work in the week ahead. Amen.

Prayer Of Confession

(Children who wish, may come forward)
Adults: O God, I have sinned against you.
Children: I turn my heart home to you.

Hymns

A Charge To Keep
O Jesus, I Have Promised
You Are Salt Of The Earth, O People

Fourth Sunday In Lent

Second Lesson: 2 Corinthians 5:16-21
Theme: Ambassadors Of Hope

Call To Worship (From Psalm 32)

Be glad in the Lord and rejoice, O righteous, and shout for joy, all you upright in heart.

Collect

Heavenly Father, we receive from you this ministry of reconciliation, because your Son came into the world not to condemn the world, but that through him the whole world should be saved! Amen.

Prayer Of Confession

Let us be reconciled to God, that we may as God's ambassadors reconcile the world. Thank you, Lord God, for your saving gospel. Amen.

Hymns

Only In Thee, O Savior Mine
Doxology
Obey My Voice

Fourth Sunday In Lent

Gospel Lesson: Luke 15:1-3, 11b-32
Theme: Treating Sinners Like Old Friends

Call To Worship

Just try to hide, people of God. God will find us. Thank God!

Collect

Lord Jesus, we are grateful for what you have taught us about forgiveness and salvation. We gather today mindful of what we have done and what we have failed to do. You have made this a place of acceptance and encouragement. Be with us today as we praise your name and resolve once more to walk in your light. How wonderful do we find your grace. Keep us on the path of salvation. These things we pray in your mighty name. Amen.

Prayer Of Confession

Lord, we stray and return, and ever you welcome us with open arms. As we consider the story of the prodigal son, we pray that we will see ourselves in the role of the prodigal, the father, and the brother. When we are weak, give us the strength to seek each other out. When we are strong, give us the spirit to welcome each other back. When we are resentful, give us the wisdom to see that you never treat any of us the same. Our joys and our concerns this morning are a sign of our varied experiences. We are grateful we are here in a place of acceptance, comfort, and encouragement, which we receive from you and from our sisters and brothers in Christ. Help us to cherish this gift. Hear our prayers, spoken and unspoken, this morning. Amen.

Hymns

Fairest Lord Jesus
What Wondrous Love Is This?
In The Cross

Fifth Sunday In Lent

First Lesson: Isaiah 43:16-21
Theme: No Reruns Here

Call To Worship (Isaiah 43:16-21)

One: Thus says the Lord, who makes a way in the sea, a path in the mighty waters,

All: who brings out chariot and horse, army and warrior; they lie down, they cannot rise, they are extinguished, quenched like a wick:

One: Do not remember the former things, or consider the things of old.

All: I am about to do a new thing; now it springs forth, do you not perceive it? I will make a way in the wilderness and rivers in the desert.

One: The wild animals will honor me, the jackals and the ostriches; for I give water in the wilderness, rivers in the desert, to give drink to my chosen people,

All: the people whom I formed for myself so that they might declare my praise.

Collect

Lord, your honor and your glory are all around us. The seasons praise you, the newborn creatures who signal the spring praise you, the skies praise you, the winds praise you. We come this morning to praise you as well, in our singing, in our speaking, in our praying. We will also speak in our silence, knowing you hear those things that are too strongly felt for words. As you plan this new thing in our midst, this resurrection that we have heard of many times, but which we have never heard of clearly until now, challenge us to be receptive to your leadings and your longings for us. Amen.

Prayer Of Confession

This day we strive, with your help, loving God, to hear each other, and to resolve to act with compassion. When there is an opportunity for ministry, we pray that you will open our hearts and energize us to action. When it is your will for us to wait, to abide in your love, to be accepting, we pray for your patience and hope. When we feel that words have abandoned us, and we struggle to speak to you, we throw ourselves upon your mercy, and repeat the words which we have learned from your Son, praying in one voice:

Our Father, who art in heaven, hallowed be thy name. Thy kingdom come. Thy will be done on earth as it is in heaven. Give us this day our daily bread, and forgive us our debts as we forgive our debtors. And lead us not into temptation, but deliver us from evil. For thine is the kingdom, the power, and the glory, forever. Amen.

Hymns

O The Unsearchable Riches
This Is A Day Of New Beginnings
Open My Eyes, That I May See

Fifth Sunday In Lent

Second Lesson: Philippians 3:4b-14
Theme: I Want To Know Christ

Call To Worship (Isaiah 43:17-18)

(Unison) I am about to do a new thing; now it springs forth, do you not perceive it? I will make a way in the wilderness and rivers in the desert.

Collect

Lord, we lay upon the altar all those things about ourselves that have become idols, and sacrifice them to you. We count it all trash compared to the grace you have offered through your Son. Transform our attitudes! Transform our lives. Amen.

Prayer Of Confession

(Children who wish, may come forward)

Adults: O God, open my eyes that I may see beyond my quick judgment, beyond my opinions and interpretations, open my eyes that I might see others,

Children: that I might see God.

Hymns

Awake, My Soul, Stretch Every Nerve
Now Go Forward
Jesus My World, My Life, My All

Fifth Sunday In Lent

Gospel Lesson: John 12:1-8
Theme: No Pleasing Some People

Call To Worship (Psalm 126)

When the Lord restored the fortunes of Zion, we were like those who dream.

Then our mouth was filled with laughter, and our tongue with shouts of joy; then it was said among the nations, "The Lord has done great things for them."

The Lord has done great things for us, and we rejoiced.

Restore our fortunes, O Lord, like the watercourses in the Negeb.

May those who sow in tears reap with shouts of joy.

Those who go out weeping, bearing the seed for sowing, shall come home with shouts of joy, carrying their sheaves.

Collect

Lord, we will never forget the one who served you while alive while other criticized. We pray that we will be remembered also as a church that serves you now by serving your world. Amen.

Prayer Of Confession

Lord, there are those who criticized the offering to your Son and our Savior. There are those who criticize our offerings as well. One of our offerings is the way we care for each other through the body of Christ. You recognize many gifts among the body of Christ, and we praise you for every opportunity we have to give. Bless our offerings today. Amen.

Hymns

O Thou Whose Gracious Presence Blest
'Tis So Sweet To Trust In Jesus
I Want Jesus To Talk With Me

Sunday Of The Passion/Palm Sunday

First Lesson: Isaiah 50:4-9a
Theme: Count Well The Cost

Call To Worship

Count the cost, sisters and brothers, so we might face the insults of the world as we follow Jesus to Golgotha and beyond.

Collect

God of sacrifice, this road to Calvary is too much for us to think about, too great a burden for us to bear. We praise you for bearing the weight of our sins for us. Today we give our offerings in memory of your redeeming love. Bless us in this time of giving. Amen.

Prayer Of Confession

(Children who wish, may come forward)

Adults: O God, in the midst of adoration, when the world loves me, and in the midst of ridicule, when the world hates me,

Children: my life is yours.

Hymns

Come, Christians, Join To Sing
Take My Life And Let It Be
Count Well The Cost *(see page 276)*

Sunday Of The Passion/Palm Sunday

Second Lesson: Philippians 2:5-11
Theme: Empty The Cup

Call To Worship

Let us empty the cup of ambition on God's altar, taking as our example our Lord Jesus, who didn't let equality with God stand in the way of service all the way to the cross.

Collect (based on Isaiah 49:8-11)

Shepherd God, in a time of favor you have answered us, on a day of salvation you have helped us; you have kept us safe, saying to us who are prisoners, "Come out," to those of us who are in darkness, "Show yourselves." You have fed us along the way. On the bare heights you have shown us pasture. Because of you we shall not hunger or thirst, neither scorching wind nor sun shall strike us down, for you have had pity on us. By springs of water you guide us. Your mountains have been turned into a road. Your highway has been raised up. You are Lord. We praise you. Amen.

Prayer Of Confession

(Children who wish, may come forward)

Adults: O God, in the midst of adoration, when the world loves me, and in the midst of ridicule, when the world hates me,

Children: my life is yours.

Hymns

All Hail The Power Of Jesus' Name (Coronation)
Fill My Cup, Lord
Man Of Sorrows

Sunday Of The Passion/Palm Sunday

Gospel Lesson: Luke 23:1-49
Theme: No. On.

Call To Worship (based on Psalm 31:9-16)

All: Be gracious to me, O Lord, for I am in distress; my eye wastes away from grief, my soul and body also.

One: For my life is spent with sorrow, and my years with sighing; my strength fails because of my misery, and my bones waste away.

Right Side: I am the scorn of all my adversaries, a horror to my neighbors, an object of dread to my acquaintances; those who see me in the street flee from me.

Left Side: I have passed out of mind like one who is dead; I have become like a broken vessel.

Women: For I hear the whispering of many — terror all around! — as they scheme together against me, as they plot to take my life.

Men: But I trust in you, O Lord; I say, "You are my God."

One: My times are in your hand; deliver me from the hand of my enemies and persecutors.

All: Let your face shine upon your servant; save me in your steadfast love.

Collect (Isaiah 50:7-8)

(Unison) The Lord God helps me; therefore I have not been disgraced; therefore I have set my face like flint, and I know that I shall not be put to shame; he who vindicates me is near.

Prayer Of Confession

Lord Jesus, we recall how the crowds adored you as you entered into Jerusalem, but also how they abandoned you at the moment of truth. We come to praise you today, recalling that glorious Palm Sunday nearly 2,000 years ago, but we come also aware of how easy it is for us to turn our backs on you as well, when others are in need, or when you have a task for us. Call us today, as we praise you, into becoming truly your people, ready for ministry, ready for service, ready for worship. Fulfill your will in our lives. Hosanna. Glory to God. Blessed are you, who come in the name of the Lord! Amen.

Hymns

Crown Him With Many Crowns
When I Survey The Wondrous Cross
Beneath The Cross Of Jesus

Maundy Thursday

First Lesson: Exodus 12:1-4 (5-10) 11-14
Theme: Who's That Knockin'?

Call To Worship (1 Thessalonians 5:16-23)

One: Rejoice always,
All: pray without ceasing,
One: give thanks in all circumstances; for this is the will of God in Christ Jesus for you.
All: Do not quench the Spirit.
One: Do not despise the words of prophets,
All: but test everything; hold fast to what is good;
One: abstain from every form of evil.
All: May the God of peace himself sanctify you entirely; and may your spirit and soul and body be kept sound and blameless at the coming of our Lord Jesus Christ.

Collect

Heavenly Father and king, we are your servants, who are nevertheless called together to share in this cup of your love. When we consider the blood of the Son who died for our sins, we marvel that you considered us worthy of this great sacrifice. You are the source of all blessing and life. This cup is offered in memory of the blessing we have received through one life lived perfectly. May we be perfected by you as well, as we do this in his memory. Amen.

Prayer Of Confession

We thank you, Lord, that you have allowed us to approach this closely to the burning bush, to sit again with the Master as he gave this example to his disciples. We praise you for the privilege of knowing Jesus Christ as risen Lord and loving servant. Help us to remember that the way to lead is to serve, the way to adore is on bended knee, the way to praise is by following your holy example. These things we pray in the name of the servant king. Amen.

Hymns

John The Revelator
Silent Night
Christ Jesus Lay

Maundy Thursday

Second Lesson: 1 Corinthians 11:23-26
Theme: Priceless

Meditation

For Christ indeed has given no special command, when or what time it should be performed, before or after supper; but he has commanded, that it should be done, and also that we should love one another, since Christ has not said that his disciples should be known by washing feet, or by the breaking of bread, but he said, "By this shall all men know, that ye are my disciples, if ye have love to one another." O how should Satan mock us justly, if we were to quarrel with each other about the time, when the feet ought to be washed; and love were destroyed, and even feet-washing and breaking of bread were altogether neglected. If our peace were thus disturbed, it would please Satan right well, and the doctrine of Jesus would be scoffed at by other men.

Therefore it is of the utmost necessity, to maintain love and peace, and to conclude to pray to our dear Lord for still more wisdom (Alexander Mack, Jr., from *The Brethren's Encyclopedia*, pp. 145-146).

Words Of Consecration

One: As often as we break this bread and drain this cup we proclaim the Lord's death until he comes.

All: We are the body of Christ. We are the lifeblood of the church, which is the bride of Christ.

One: In the manner of our living we make visible the kingdom of Jesus in the present world.

All: The body of Christ dwells within us all. The blood of Christ, given freely for our transgressions, flows in our veins.

One: In this renewal of the drama of our salvation we demonstrate the assurance of the world to come.

All: Christ has died. Christ is risen. Christ will come again!

Words To Take With You As We Go

(from 1 Corinthians 1:20-24)

Where is the one who is wise? Where is the scribe? Where is the debater of this age? Has not God made foolish the wisdom of the world? For since, in the wisdom of God, the world did not know God through wisdom, God decided, through the foolishness of our proclamation, to save those who believe. For Jews demand signs and Greeks desire wisdom, but we proclaim Christ crucified, a stumbling block to Jews and foolishness to Gentiles, but to those who are the called, both Jews and Greeks, Christ the power of God and the wisdom of God.

Hymns

Let Us Break Bread Together
Here In This Place
Here In This Upper Room

Maundy Thursday

Gospel Lesson: John 13:1-17, 31b-35
Theme: Why Is This Night So Different?

Call To Worship

One: Why is this night so different from all others?

All: Tonight we seek with God's grace to answer the question, "What would Jesus do?"

One: Why is this night the same as all others?

All: The call of Jesus Christ is the same — to bend the knee in service to each other, to break bread in fellowship, and to drain the cup in remembrance of the Lord's death, until he returns.

One And All: Come, let us gather together in the name of Jesus the Christ, Lord and Savior, sharing this communion with believers around the world.

Collect

Lord, bless us as we gather together in your name, following your example, as we strive to serve your people. We will take hold of the salvation that we share, cherishing the precious gift of your words and deeds, and imperfectly imitate your perfection. For your example, and for the example of your servants who have reflected your light for our benefit, we give you thanks and praise. Amen!

Prayer Of Confession

Bless this meal, Lord, we pray, and grace us with your presence, unseen as you dwell in our midst, and visible in our sisters and brothers who have in turn graced us with their presence. Nourish us physically and spiritually as we resolve once more to live your will in this present world, and in the world to come. Amen.

Hymns

Here In This Place
O Let All Who Thirst
Let Us Break Bread Together

Good Friday

First Lesson: Isaiah 52:13—53:12
Theme: Vindication. Trust Me.

Call To Worship (built around Isaiah 53:1-6)

(Unison) You can run, but you can't hide.

Who has believed what we have heard? And to whom has the arm of the Lord been revealed? For he grew up before him like a young plant, and like a root out of dry ground; he had no form or majesty that we should look at him, nothing in his appearance that we should desire him. He was despised and rejected by others; a man of suffering and acquainted with infirmity; and as one from whom others hide their faces he was despised, and we held him of no account. Surely he has borne our infirmities and carried our diseases; yet we accounted him stricken, struck down by God, and afflicted. But he was wounded for our transgressions, crushed for our iniquities; upon him was the punishment that made us whole, and by his bruises we are healed. All we like sheep have gone astray; we have all turned to our own way, and the Lord has laid on him the iniquity of us all.

You can hide, but you cannot run....

Collect

We thank you, Lord, for hiding this vision from us much of the time, so we may walk in your world in purpose and not paralyzed by horror. May the sight of your crucified Son galvanize us so that we will go willingly into your world to eliminate suffering and bring light to dark places in your name. Amen.

Prayer Of Confession

Lord, into your hands we deliver our sins.
Lord, from your hands we receive forgiveness. Amen.

Hymns

Alas, And Did My Savior Bleed
Jesus, Keep Me Near The Cross
What Wondrous Love Is This?

Good Friday

Second Lesson: Hebrews 4:14-16; 5:7-9
Theme: Approach ...

Call To Worship

On August 27, 1883, James Wallis, chief of police on Rodriguez Island, not far from Zanzibar, wrote: "Several times during the night (26-27) reports were heard coming from the eastward, like the distant roar of heavy guns. These reports continued at intervals of between three and four hours, until 3 p.m. on the 27th, and the last two were heard in the directions of Oyster Bay and Port Mathurie." What Wallis was hearing were the distant eruptions of the Volcano Krakatoa, 2,968 miles away. There is no recorded instance in human history of a sound being heard from further away.

Except, of course, the echoes of that hammer driving in the nails on a hill far away, on Golgotha.

Collect

We can do no other, Lord, except to watch and wait. May we, with the strength of the women who did not abandon you, watch and wait with you this time as well. Amen.

Prayer Of Confession

Lord, we thirst for answers. We are parched, with cracked throats, as we think of your misery and the misery of others. We need you. Do not leave us now. Lord, we follow. Amen.

Hymns

When I Survey The Wondrous Cross
Ride On, Ride On In Majesty
Go To Dark Gethsemane

Good Friday

Gospel Lesson: John 18:1—19:42
Theme: You Are Here

Call To Worship

Two wooden beams: a four by four post fourteen feet high and a two by four crossbar — total: $9

Three spikes — 24 cents

Hemp rope — $5.95 for a fifty-foot coil

Dice to roll for castoff clothing — 95 cents

Real life in Christ — priceless

For most of what life offers us, there is cash and credit.

For everything that really matters, there's the cross of Jesus.

Collect

Stay with us, Lord, through the Golgothas of our lives. Do not abandon us as we have abandoned you. Amen.

Prayer Of Confession

Pilate asked, "What is truth?" This is truth. Jesus died on the cross. Jesus died for us. Jesus saves us. And there's this thing about the empty tomb that we're going to tell you about in just a couple of days. Truth. There is truth. God is truth. Amen.

Hymns

Stay With Me
Just As I Am
The Old Rugged Cross

The Resurrection Of Our Lord/Easter Day

First Lesson: Acts 10:34-43
Theme: Thank Heavens I Don't Get No Respect!

Call To Worship (Isaiah 65:17-25)

One: [The Lord says] For I am about to create new heavens and a new earth; the former things shall not be remembered or come to mind.

All: But be glad and rejoice forever in what I am creating; for I am about to create Jerusalem as a joy, and its people as a delight.

One: I will rejoice in Jerusalem, and delight in my people; no more shall the sound of weeping be heard in it, or the cry of distress.

All: No more shall there be in it an infant that lives but a few days, or an old person who does not live out a lifetime; for one who dies at a hundred years will be considered a youth, and one who falls short of a hundred will be considered accursed.

One: They shall build houses and inhabit them; they shall plant vineyards and eat their fruit.

All: They shall not build and another inhabit; they shall not plant and another eat; for like the days of a tree shall the days of my people be, and my chosen shall long enjoy the work of their hands.

One: They shall not labor in vain, or bear children for calamity; for they shall be offspring blessed by the Lord — and their descendants as well.

All: Before they call I will answer, while they are yet speaking I will hear.

One: The wolf and the lamb shall feed together, the lion shall eat straw like the ox; but the serpent — its food shall be dust! They shall not hurt or destroy on all my holy mountain, says the Lord.

Collect

Lord, once more we come together to tell again the story of the resurrection. Christ the Lord is risen today. Christ is risen indeed. Told and retold, this central fact of our faith never fails to amaze us. You amaze us, Lord, with your goodness and your mercy. This day resurrect within us our hopes and our dreams, that we may take this good news, this gospel, to the nations. We praise you. We thank you. Amen.

Prayer Of Confession

This is our confession which we make today. All the boundaries and borders we create between people are false and fallen. God does not care about our categories. We are all God's children, and we will pray for our enemies as well as our friends, seek ceaselessly for the fallen, and open the circle ever wider until all are one in God.

Hymns

Come Ye Faithful, Raise The Strain
Now The Green Blade Rises
Christ The Lord Is Risen Today

The Resurrection Of Our Lord/Easter Day

Second Lesson: 1 Corinthians 15:19-26
Theme: More To Be Pitied Than Envied

Call To Worship

He is risen! He is risen indeed!

Collect

We are not smug, Lord Jesus, but certain of this: You have died, you are risen, you will come again! Amen.

Prayer Of Confession

Our offerings today pale in comparison to the glory of your gift to us, in the person of our risen Lord. Even so, we come bearing these offerings, as a token of our obedience and a pledge of our desire to serve you this day and every day. Amen.

Hymns

The Strife Is O'er
They Crucified My Savior (He Arose)
Thine Is The Glory

The Resurrection Of Our Lord/Easter Day

Gospel Lesson: John 20:1-18
Theme: Ha!

Call To Worship (based on Psalm 118:1-2, 14-24)

One: O give thanks to the Lord, for he is good; his steadfast love endures forever!

All: Let God's people say, "His steadfast love endures forever."

Right Side: The Lord is my strength and my might.

Left Side: He has become my salvation.

Men: I shall not die, but I shall live, and recount the deeds of the Lord.

Women: The Lord has punished me severely, but he did not give me over to death.

Upstairs: The stone that the builders rejected has become the chief cornerstone.

Downstairs: This is the Lord's doing; it is marvelous in our eyes.

All: This is the day that the Lord has made; let us rejoice and be glad in it.

Collect

Lord of new life, God of resurrection, as we walk in that garden today, may we feel once more the surprise, the shock, the joy that comes with the unexpected, yet long-predicted, glory of our happy ending with you. All praise and glory to your name. Amen.

Prayer Of Confession

Today on Easter, God of good gifts, our joys are even more joyful. Today on Easter, God of comfort, our sorrows, though real, sting less because our hope has been realized in the resurrection. We once more resolve to become your people, to minister to each other, and to a needy world. Hear us today. Answer our prayers swiftly. These things we pray in the name of Jesus, who is risen. Amen.

Hymns

How Firm A Foundation
Low In Grave He Lay
Christ The Lord Is Risen Today

Second Sunday Of Easter

First Lesson: Acts 5:27-32
Theme: We Are Witnesses Of God's Love

Call To Worship

Grace to you and peace, from the Alpha and the Omega, to whom all belongs, and who shares with all.

Collect

Lord of all things, bless us as we learn to share in mutual aid and love those things you have blessed us with and put into our hands for this time, before they are returned to you for all time. Amen.

Prayer Of Confession (based on Job 1:21)

We bring nothing into this world and we take nothing away from it. Blessed be your name, Lord, for the opportunities we have to disperse your blessings among all people. Amen.

Hymns

We Are People Of God's Peace
Christ Is Risen! Shout Hosanna
Blest Be The Tie That Binds

Second Sunday Of Easter

Second Lesson: Revelation 1:4-8
Theme: Will The Real Jesus Please Stand Up!

Call To Worship (Psalm 150)

One: Praise the Lord! Praise God in his sanctuary; praise him in his mighty firmament!

All: Praise him for his mighty deeds; praise him according to his surpassing greatness!

One: Praise him with trumpet sound; praise him with lute and harp!

All: Praise him with tambourine and dance; praise him with strings and pipe!

One: Praise him with clanging cymbals; praise him with loud clashing cymbals!

All: Let everything that breathes praise the Lord! Praise the Lord!

Collect

Lord, we offer up to you the music of our heart, the notes of our soul, the lyrics of our lives. Be present with us today, conducting our thoughts and intentions, leading us in our worship. You are the source, you are the author, of all that is best in us. When we become your will then we allow your light that is in us to shine in the darkest corners of the world. We praise you. We adore you. Amen!

Prayer Of Confession

Alpha and Omega, first and last, the whole of creation, all that we see, and all that is hidden from our sight, is yours by virtue of the fact that you made it. The earth is yours, and the fullness thereof. What we offer is a token of that fullness. Accept it as an earnest of greater things to come. Increase our dedication to your work and your kingdom. Amen.

Hymns

I See A New World Coming
Oh, How Wondrous The Grace
It Is Well With My Soul

Second Sunday Of Easter

Gospel Lesson: John 20:19-31
Theme: Believing Thomas

Call To Worship (Psalm 118:17)

(Unison) I shall not die, but I shall live, and recount the deeds of the Lord.

Collect (John 20:28)

(Unison) My Lord and my God!

Prayer Of Confession (John 20:30-31)

One: Now Jesus did many other signs in the presence of his disciples, which are not written in this book.

All: But these are written so that you may come to believe that Jesus is the Messiah, the Son of God, and that through believing you may have life in his name.

Hymns

Because He Lives
How Majestic Is Your Name
This Joyful Eastertide

Third Sunday Of Easter

First Lesson: Acts 9:1-6 (7-20)
Theme: Real Change In Real People

Call To Worship (based on Revelation 5:11-14)

One: When John the Revelator looked, he heard the voice of many angels surrounding the throne and the living creatures and the elders; they numbered myriads of myriads and thousands of thousands, singing with full voice:

Women: "Worthy is the Lamb that was slaughtered to receive power and wealth and wisdom and might and honor and glory and blessing!"

Men: Then John heard every creature in heaven and on earth and under the earth and in the sea, and all that is in them, singing:

Right Side: "To the one seated on the throne and to the Lamb be blessing and honor and glory and might forever and ever!"

Left Side: And the four living creatures said:

All: "Amen!"

One: And God's people worshiped.

Collect

Worthy are you, Lord, to claim everything in heaven and on earth. Worthy are you, Lord, to claim us as well. As we gather for worship we pray that we will hear your call in the singing, the speaking, the preaching, the reading, and in the silences between the words and the notes of the music. Amen.

Prayer Of Confession

Lord, whatever it takes to change our lives, even after the manner of Paul your servant, Lord, whatever it takes, we ask, gritting our teeth, that you will do to claim us, to change us, to transform us into your witnessing people. Amen.

Hymns

O Worship The King
Sing Hallelujah, Praise The Lord
Oh, For A Thousand Tongues To Sing

Third Sunday Of Easter

Second Lesson: Revelation 5:11-14
Theme: Now That's Entertainment

Call To Worship

Welcome to God's musical, the book of Revelation, where the redeemed break out in song, pain and suffering is over, and the story has no end!

Collect

Lord, there are so many signs of your wonder and glory all about us, in things seen and unseen. But in our midst this day we see your people, gathered together from all walks of life, ill and well, tired and rejuvenated, dutiful and spiritual — and this is wonder enough for us, that you are in our midst. We praise you this morning. Guide us in your worship. Worthy are you! Blessing and honor and glory and might be yours forever and ever! Amen.

Prayer Of Confession

Your martyrs suffered terribly, Lord of life, but their suffering is over and their crown is eternal. Help us keep our eyes on the prize as well as we endure suffering for your sake and for the good news. Amen.

Hymns

Blessing And Honor And Glory
Sleepers, Wake!
Come Away To The Skies

Third Sunday Of Easter

Gospel Lesson: John 21:1-19
Theme: Love Story

Call To Worship

God knows that we love him, but the world may not. Gather in worship, and gather strength for the task of witnessing to the world about our Savior!

Collect

With heart and hands we offer to you today a gift of praise and worship, in memory of the love you have given freely to us, Lord. Amen.

Prayer Of Confession

We thank you, Jesus, that you will listen to us on our terms and not your own, and that when we fail to measure up to the difficult task of discipleship you are willing to accept us and use us anyway. Amen.

Hymns

Come Thou Font Of Every Blessing
My Jesus, I Love Thee
Where Cross The Crowded Ways Of Life

Fourth Sunday Of Easter

First Lesson: Acts 9:36-43
Theme: What We Really Miss

Call To Worship

Let us call to mind those who have loved the Lord, who the Lord has called home. In loving the Lord we may always love them as well. Live in the Lord. Love the Lord. Love all.

Collect

Lord who made all, we thank you for all those we have come to know, for the ways in which they reflect your majesty, for the part they have played in our lives. Even so, in our worship this day we seek to put you first; you who are worthy of all our love. Let us never lose sight of you, nor fail to see others in your light. Amen.

Prayer Of Confession

God of power and majesty, each person you have made is precious beyond price, and worthy of the priceless salvation that comes through the sacrifice of your Son. Help us to look beyond what a person can do for us, and to see them as you see them. Amen.

Hymns

God Of The Earth, The Sky, The Sea
Spirit Of God, Descend Upon My Heart
God Of Grace And God Of Glory

Fourth Sunday Of Easter

Second Lesson: Revelation 7:9-17
Theme: Two Ways Of Looking

Call To Worship (based on Revelation 7:9-10)

One: Salvation belongs to our God who is seated on the throne, and to the Lamb!

All: Amen! Blessing and glory and wisdom and thanksgiving and honor and power and might be to our God for ever and ever! Amen.

Collect

Lamb of God, shepherd us past the temptations of this world so that we too may stand before the throne to give you praise and honor forever and ever. Amen.

Prayer Of Confession

What a joyful sound we have heard this morning, when our people rise to share their happiness. What sorrow we share, when our concerns are shared. Lord, you have numbered every hair on our head. No sparrow falls unnoticed. We count upon your mercy, and your swift answer to our prayers. We are thankful as well that you expect us to respond to the distress of your children. These things we pray in your glorious name, calling to mind always the words which we were taught by your Son, and our Savior, saying in one voice: Our Father, who art in heaven, hallowed be thy name. Thy kingdom come. Thy will be done on earth as it is in heaven. Give us this day our daily bread, and forgive us our debts, as we forgive our debtors, and lead us not into temptation, but deliver us from evil. For thine is the kingdom, the power, and the glory forever. Amen.

Hymns

Jesus Christ, God's Only Son *(see page 278)*
Hosanna, Loud Hosanna
The Lord's My Shepherd

Fourth Sunday Of Easter

Gospel Lesson: John 10:22-30
Theme: I Know This Guy!

Call To Worship (Psalm 23 KJV)

The Lord is my shepherd; I shall not want. He maketh me to lie down in green pastures: he leadeth me beside the still waters. He restoreth my soul: he leadeth me in the paths of righteousness for his name's sake. Yea, though I walk through the valley of the shadow of death, I will fear no evil: for thou art with me; thy rod and thy staff they comfort me. Thou preparest a table before me in the presence of mine enemies: thou anointest my head with oil; my cup runneth over. Surely goodness and mercy shall follow me all the days of my life: and I will dwell in the house of the Lord for ever.

Collect

Gentle shepherd, unseen but always present, we gather together and confess our need for your guidance. Lead us in our worship today, and then lead us beyond our worship into service in your name for your world. Your goodness and mercy uphold us. Your care for us astounds us. Your faithfulness in the natural world and in our lives sustains us. We praise you. We worship you. Amen.

Prayer Of Confession

This day we offer to you a measure of our wealth, confessing that in comparison to the rest of the world our wealth is our shame. Let this fact challenge us to examine the offering of our lives that we give to you as well. These things we pray in the name of the risen Lord. Amen.

Hymns

Gentle Shepherd
The King Of Love My Shepherd Is
All Hail The Power Of Jesus' Name (Diadem)

Fifth Sunday Of Easter

First Lesson: Acts 11:1-18
Theme: We Should Love One Another

Call To Worship

Let us listen this day not only to God, but to each other, in the words that are spoken and the expressions that speak even more loudly. Let us come to know God through the precious gift of our sisters and brothers. Then we shall come to know God.

Collect

God of word and speech, we thank you for the ways in which we can express ourselves, and pray that our expressions of praise will be received in an even greater manner than our hearts intend. Amen.

Prayer Of Confession

Lord, how often do we fail to truly listen to our sisters and brothers when we speak together? We finish a sentence before it is completed, categorize and ignore our family of faith, put people into boxes labeled by age or ethnicity, or simply become so preoccupied with ourselves that we lose sight of you in the process. You have blessed us with a family of faith. May we grow worthy of the gift. Amen.

Hymns

Holy Manna
Help Us To Help Each Other
Blest Be The Tie

Fifth Sunday Of Easter

Second Lesson: Revelation 21:1-6
Theme: It's About Time

Call To Worship

See, people of God, the new heaven and the new earth, begging to burst through that which we imagine to be solid and enduring. Ignore illusions today and set your hearts and minds upon God's great destiny that we are to share.

Collect

God of glory, we praise you for the glory we see all around us as we gather together for worship. Send your Spirit to dwell among us in our praying, in our praising, in our raising of song. Send us the peace that passes understanding, and the joy that sustains us in all circumstances. Amen.

Prayer Of Confession

At the round earth's imagined corners, blow
Your trumpets, Angels, and arise, arise
From death, you numberless infinities
Of souls, and to your scattered bodies go,
All whom the flood did, and fire shall o'erthrow,
All whom war, dearth, age, agues, tyrannies,
Despair, law, chance, hath slain, and you whose eyes
Shall behold God, and never taste death's woe.
But let them sleep, Lord, and me mourn a space
For, if above all these my sins abound
'Tis late to ask abundance of thy grace
When we are there; here on this lowly ground
Teach me how to repent, for that's as good
As if thou hadst seal'd my pardon, with my blood.

— John Donne, *Holy Sonnets*

Hymns

New Earth, Heavens New
Soon And Very Soon
I Love To Tell The Story

Fifth Sunday Of Easter

Gospel Lesson: John 13:31-35
Theme: Just So You're Sure

Call To Worship (Psalm 148:1-6)

Praise the Lord! Praise the Lord from the heavens; praise him in the heights!

Praise him, all his angels; praise him, all his host!

Praise him, sun and moon; praise him, all you shining stars!

Praise him, you highest heavens, and you waters above the heavens!

Let them praise the name of the Lord, for he commanded and they were created.

He established them forever and ever; he fixed their bounds, which cannot be passed.

Collect

We thank you, God of love, for the instruction you gave your disciples, admonishing them — and us — to love as you have loved. May we do so in worship today and in our life of worship every day. Amen.

Prayer Of Confession

Jesus gave us a command, to love one another as he loved us. By this the world is to recognize us as Christians. Oh, Lord, how often do we claim to be Christians, yet fail to demonstrate this love with one another? No more. We shall strive to be your people, so that by the manner of our living others may come to know your love as well. Amen.

Hymns

They'll Know We Are Christians By Our Love
Will You Let Me Be Your Servant?
I Love Thy Kingdom, Lord

Sixth Sunday Of Easter

First Lesson: Acts 16:9-15
Theme: A Dream For Salvation

Call To Worship

Come! We are called, not only by God, but by God's hurting people. Come! Let us worship the God of love in truth.

Collect

As you called the Apostle Paul to untold hardships and victory through a dream, so we hope to be called as well by any means you choose into service and ministry, through our time of worship together, and beyond. Amen.

Prayer Of Confession

Do you hear God calling? Does God call us away from comfort and toward ministry and service? Let us ignore God's call in worship and prayer, and seek to save ourselves alone. Let us hide within these four walls, and preserve ourselves away from adventure and calling, let us close our ears to the God who calls from the four corners of the globe, let us insulate ourselves from the world and wrap ourselves in our prejudices. Let us cling to easy answers and generalizations for the difficult problems God presents us, and let us fail to love our enemies and demonize those who disagree with us. Let us listen to those who call us to fear and who seek to confirm our ignorance and hopelessness, and who do this in the name of the God of love.

Who will say, "Amen," to this prayer?

(silence)

Who will, as Paul, listen to God calling far beyond our comfort zone instead?

Hymns

Lift Every Voice And Sing
Wade In The Water
Here In This Place

Sixth Sunday Of Easter

Second Lesson: Revelation 21:10, 22—22:5
Theme: Game Over

Call To Worship

Open the doors of our church, as the doors of the new Jerusalem remain open. Let all come in here that all may be welcomed there in the beyond!

Collect

We humbly come to worship you, ever mindful of the river of goodness which flows from your throne, inundating us with more blessings than we can thank you for, or even imagine. Amen.

Prayer Of Confession

Children: The Lord God will reign forever and ever!

Hymns

No Night There
Good Night And Good Morning
Oh, Holy City Seen Of John

Sixth Sunday Of Easter

Gospel Lesson: John 14:23-29
Theme: I Need A Hero

Call To Worship (Psalm 67)

May God be gracious to us and bless us and make his face to shine upon us, *Selah*, that your way may be known upon earth, your saving power among all nations. Let the peoples praise you, O God; let all the peoples praise you. Let the nations be glad and sing for joy, for you judge the peoples with equity and guide the nations upon earth. *Selah* Let the peoples praise you, O God; let all the peoples praise you. The earth has yielded its increase; God, our God, has blessed us. May God continue to bless us; let all the ends of the earth revere him.

Collect

Lord, you have served us in so many ways, beyond count, beyond measure, beyond knowledge. We strive to serve you, but you are perfect and self-sufficient, needing nothing. Your salvation is a free gift, and you ask nothing in return. In response, we pledge again to serve others, asking nothing in return, in imitation of your mercy and goodness. Be present with us this morning. Heal us as your people. Amen.

Prayer Of Confession

Lord, hear our prayers. Hear our prayers as they were spoken, shared with the community of faith. Lord hear our prayers. Hear our prayers which were silently raised in the midst of the community, those things felt too deeply to be shared aloud, but in need of your intervention as surely as those petitions shared aloud. Lord, hear our prayers, hear those prayers which we have not yet raised to you, aloud or silently. Lord, we believe. Help our unbelief. Amen.

Hymns

Art Thou Wearied, Art Thou Troubled?
Peace, Perfect Peace
Hidden Peace

The Ascension Of Our Lord

First Lesson: Acts1:1-11
Theme: View From A Height

Call To Worship

Close your eyes. Think of Jesus on that hill. Hold on to his hand. Rise with him. See the ground fall away. Let go of your fears. Reach for the skies. Adore Jesus. The door is Jesus. Come in. Come. Now is the time to worship.

Collect

Lord Jesus, we proclaim you risen and present, alive and active, and ready to return. We pray we will be ready as well, and while we wait we hope to fulfill your command to take the gospel to the ends of the earth. Bless us not only as we support the missions of the church, both near at hand and far away, but as we get actively involved as well. Amen.

Prayer Of Confession (based on Acts 1:11 and 8)

Christians, why do you stand looking up toward heaven? This Jesus, who has been taken up from you into heaven, will come in the same way as you saw him go into heaven. Let us receive power from the Holy Spirit and become witnesses of Christ in Jerusalem, in all Judea and Samaria, and to the ends of the earth.

Hymns

Come, Now Is The Time To Worship
Spirit Divine, Inspire Our Prayers
Hear The Voice Of Jesus Say

The Ascension Of Our Lord

Second Lesson: Ephesians 1:15-23
Theme: That's Him!

Call To Worship (based on Ephesians 1:18-21)

Let us open the eyes of our hearts, so we may come to know the hope to which we have been called, the riches of our glorious inheritance, and the Christ whom God raised from the dead, who is seated at the right hand in glory, who reigns above every ruler and authority, every power and dominion, now and forever!

Collect

Amen! Amen! We serve you, risen Lord! Amen! Amen! We live your holy Word!

Prayer Of Confession

This is our hope, this is our certainty, that Jesus is Lord and reigns above all things on earth, and that everything that has been made has been placed beneath his feet, that all will be well, and that all manner of things will be well. Amen! Amen!

Hymns

Amen!
Crown Him With Many Crowns
God Is Working His Purpose Out

The Ascension Of Our Lord

Gospel Lesson: Luke 24:44-53
Theme: Why Do We Wonder?

Call To Worship

Rise, people of God, in worship, as you are able, as Jesus was able to rise from the sight of his apostles, but never out of sight from our hearts.

Collect

Do not forget us, Lord Jesus, in your kingdom, but watch over us and bless us this day and every day, until you return, in power and glory, and in the sight of all. Amen.

Prayer Of Confession (based on Luke 24:46-48)

Jesus, the Messiah, suffered and died and rose from the dead on the third. We must preach the repentance for the forgiveness of sins to all nations, beginning close to home and spreading throughout the world. We are witnesses of these things.

Hymns

See The Splendor Of The Morning
Sing We Triumphant Hymns
Look, You Saints, The Sight Is Glorious

Seventh Sunday Of Easter

First Lesson: Acts 16:16-34
Theme: What Must We Do To Be Saved?

Call To Worship

If we must suffer, let it be for Jesus. If we are mocked, let it be for the Lord. If we are excluded, or hunted, or cast out from the midst of friends and family, let it be because our service to God upsets the comfortable order and calls all to repentance and service! Let us be God's people today.

Collect

Be present with us, Lord, today,
In all your minister might say,
In all your songs call from our heart,
In all your children's scribbled art.
In all the adults' restlessness,
In what our soul-struck hearts confess,
That all may call upon you, Lord,
And share our comfort in your Word.

Prayer Of Confession

Lord, we are the jailers. Our sisters and brothers in the third world, who grow and pick our food, sew our clothing, make our consumer goods, for mere pennies in horrible conditions, are our prisoners. We have mistreated them, as the jailer mistreated Paul. Shake our lives with a spiritual earthquake, set us all free so that we may no longer ignore them, but treat all as sisters and brothers in Christ. What must we do to be saved? Let us treat the least of these as you and as your ambassadors. Amen.

Hymns

Comfort, Comfort, O My People
Precious Lord
What A Friend We Have In Jesus

Seventh Sunday Of Easter

Second Lesson: Revelation 22:12-14, 16-17, 20-21
Theme: A Promise Is A Promise

Call To Worship

Believe on the Lord Jesus, and you will be saved.

Collect

Come, Lord Jesus. Come soon, Jesus, root and offspring of David, and the bright morning star. Alpha and Omega, first and last, beginning and end. Amen. Come, Lord Jesus.

Prayer Of Confession (from Revelation 22:21)

May the grace of the Lord Jesus be with all of God's people! Amen.

Hymns

Of The Father's Love Begotten
Morning Star, O Cheering Sight!
Christ Is Coming! Let Creation

Seventh Sunday Of Easter

Gospel Lesson: John 17:20-26
Theme: That We May All Be One

Call To Worship (Psalm 97:1, 12)

The Lord is king! Let the earth rejoice; let the many coastlands be glad!
Rejoice in the Lord, O you righteous, and give thanks to his holy name!

Collect

Gracious God of creation, what could be more glorious than the flowers of spring, the greedy grass reaching for the sun, the fields coming to life after the hard work of the farmer and the gardener. There is glory enough for us all around us. Yet you have also blessed us with the spark of your Spirit, that enables us to see beyond that which is before us, to your greater glory beyond us. Inspire us in our worship today, so we might learn to put the heavenly above the worldly, while keeping in mind that you are the author of both. Bless us in our worship today. Amen.

Prayer Of Confession

Lord, we have listened to each other's words this morning during our time of sharing. Help us to hear beyond the words to the things that are unsaid. We know you have heard our earnest entreaties, both spoken and unspoken. Plant in our hearts your wisdom now so that we may be able to respond to those in need, both those in our midst, and those in the wider world. Amen.

Hymns

Christ Has Arisen, Alleluia!
How Good A Thing It Is
Built On The Rock

The Day Of Pentecost

First Lesson: Acts 2:1-21
Theme: Clarity!

Call To Worship (based on Psalm 104:24-35)

O Lord, how manifold are your works! In wisdom you have made them all; the earth is full of your creatures.

Yonder is the sea, great and wide, creeping things innumerable are there, living things both small and great.

There go the ships, and Leviathan that you formed to sport in it.

These all look to you to give them their food in due season;

when you give to them, they gather it up; when you open your hand, they are filled with good things.

When you hide your face, they are dismayed; when you take away their breath, they die and return to their dust.

When you send forth your Spirit, they are created; and you renew the face of the ground. May the glory of the Lord endure forever; may the Lord rejoice in his works —

who looks on the earth and it trembles, who touches the mountains and they smoke.

I will sing to the Lord as long as I live; I will sing praise to my God while I have being.

May my meditation be pleasing to him, for I rejoice in the Lord.

Bless the Lord, O my soul. Praise the Lord!

Collect

Lord God, you spoke with power when you made the world. You spoke with clarity when the Word was made flesh and dwelt among us. You carved out a new people when your Spirit descended in our midst at Pentecost. We call to mind today your transforming power. Sweep us away despite our native caution. Create again your people, driven by your Spirit. Amen.

Prayer Of Confession

Set on us fire, Spirit of God! Brighten our hearts with the love of God that called forth the universe in all its majesty for God's own pleasure and our own. Inspire us with the glory of the world we can only guess at, too small to be observed unaided, yet essential to our well being. Sharpen the sense of glory our own bodies should inspire, temples of the living God, alive with God's purpose! Move in our midst! Amen.

Hymns

Revive Us Again!
O Holy Spirit, Making Whole
Move In Our Midst *(see page 280)*

The Day Of Pentecost

Second Lesson: Romans 8:14-17
Theme: No Fear

Call To Worship (Romans 8:14-17)

One: For all who are led by the Spirit of God are children of God.

All: For you did not receive a spirit of slavery to fall back into fear, but you have received a spirit of adoption. When we cry, "Abba! Father!"

One: it is that very Spirit bearing witness with our spirit that we are children of God,

All: and if children, then heirs, heirs of God and joint heirs with Christ — if, in fact, we suffer with him so that we may also be glorified with him.

Collect

We praise you, mighty Spirit, for the adoption we have received, and we seek to bear witness to your power and glory. Abba! Father! Amen.

Prayer Of Confession

Though we are surrounded by a host of troubles, we will not fear, for you are our Heavenly Father, Abba, and we are, through you, heirs of God and joint heirs with Christ! Amen.

Hymns

Joys Are Flowing
This Is My Father's World
Ask Ye What Great Thing

The Day Of Pentecost

Gospel Lesson: John 14:8-17 (25-27)
Theme: Choose

Call To Worship

One: What shall we choose — Babel or the Spirit?

All: The world offers Babel, the senseless lure of possessions and worldly power.

Right Side: The Spirit rushes in like a mighty wind,

Left Side: transforming God's people so we speak as one and hear as one.

One: Babel beckons, but the Spirit is patient.

All: Lord, call us to be your people today.

Collect

Lord, we believe that your Spirit is still present and active among your people. We pray that this Spirit, which always abides with us, can be made manifest through us to the world, that all may call upon your name and be saved. Let your will be done on earth as it is perfectly performed in heaven. Let Pentecost sweep us again into your service, as you have willed through all of your history. These things we pray in the name of the risen Christ. Amen.

Prayer Of Confession

Let us build a tower of prayer and praise, not to our own glory, but to God's glory, that all may see it and not see us. Let us hem this building about with song and celebration, that all who enter will see God's presence and rise to glory. Let your Spirit speak past our words so that we may fully understand the extent of your love for us, in Christ Jesus our Lord. Let your kingdom become present in our lives in this tower of praise and prayer, according to your will. Amen.

Hymns

The God Of Abraham Praise
Breathe On Me, Breath Of God
O Holy Spirit, Making Whole

The Holy Trinity

First Lesson: Proverbs 8:1-4, 22-31
Theme: Roll Call

Call To Worship

Listen. God is calling you. God is calling you in wisdom. Listen. Learn. Love.

Collect

God of wisdom, God of calling, we see your solid planning in the world around us, and the sense of your plan in the universe on display. We pray that your wisdom will find a home in our hearts as well. Amen.

Prayer Of Confession

Adults: Blest be the tie that binds.
Children: God be with you till we meet again.

Hymns

Praise To The Lord, The Almighty
Blest Be The Tie That Binds
God Be With You Till We Meet Again

The Holy Trinity

Second Lesson: Romans 5:1-5
Theme: SST (Serious Spiritual Training)

Call To Worship

Come, God's people, let us gather with firm intent to live not just as believers, but as disciples.

Collect

God who challenges, we praise for strength to answer your call. Amen.

Prayer Of Confession (based on Romans 5:1-5)

Lord, we have brought before you our joys and our concerns, your hellos and our good-byes. Unspoken, yet present, are emotions deeply felt but hard to express, as we take our leave of each other for a time. We are assured that you are with us through all our trials. Therefore, since we are justified by faith, we have peace with God through our Lord Jesus Christ, through whom we have obtained access to this grace in which we stand; and we boast in our hope of sharing the glory of God. Not only that, but we also boast in our sufferings, that suffering produces endurance, and endurance produces character, and character produces hope, and hope does not disappoint us, because God's love has been poured into our hearts through the Holy Spirit that has been given to us. So we pray with boldness, knowing you hear us, as we approach the throne of grace with the words we learned from your Son and our Savior, saying in one voice: Our Father, who art in heaven, hallowed be thy name. Thy kingdom come, thy will be done, on earth as it is in heaven. Give us this day our daily bread, and forgive us our debts, as we forgive our debtors. And lead us not into temptation, but deliver us from evil. For thine is the kingdom, the power, and the glory, forever. Amen.

Hymns

Sweet Hour Of Prayer
Amazing Grace
Go Forth With God's Blessing

The Holy Trinity

Gospel Lesson: John 16:12-15
Theme: Much More To Say

Call To Worship (Psalm 8)

Women: O Lord, our Sovereign, how majestic is your name in all the earth! You have set your glory above the heavens.

Men: Out of the mouths of babes and infants you have founded a bulwark because of your foes, to silence the enemy and the avenger.

Right Side: When I look at your heavens, the work of your fingers, the moon and the stars that you have established;

Left Side: what are human beings that you are mindful of them, mortals that you care for them?

Upstairs: Yet you have made them a little lower than God, and crowned them with glory and honor.

Downstairs: You have given them dominion over the works of your hands; you have put all things under their feet,

Younger: all sheep and oxen, and also the beasts of the field,

Older: the birds of the air, and the fish of the sea, whatever passes along the paths of the seas.

One: O Lord, our Sovereign, how majestic is your name in all the earth!

Collect

Protect us, Lord, as we wait for your Spirit to move in our midst once more. Bless us as we receive your living Word. Amen.

Prayer Of Confession

Living God, so often we seek to silence you, hemming you in within the pages of a book, as if we could control you, and prevent you from speaking through our children, our seniors, through the women and men in our midst. Open our hearts, our minds, our hands, so we might hear your Spirit, understand you, and work diligently for your kingdom. Amen.

Hymns

Sweet Hour Of Prayer
This Is The Threefold Truth
Will You Let Me Be Your Servant?

Proper 4/Ordinary Time 9
Sunday between May 29 and June 4 inclusive

First Lesson: 1 Kings 18:20-21 (22-29) 30-39
Theme: The Right Way To Make Trouble

Call To Worship

The Lord is God! There is no other! Be glad in the Lord and rejoice!

Collect

Lord, accept the offering of our hearts as we seek you in this, your holy place. Amen.

Prayer Of Confession

God of Israel, God of all nations, there is idolatry all around us, and especially within us. Our families, our nation, our jobs, our avocations, all these good things come from you, but when we put them before you we create idols as powerful as ever in the history of your people. May we worship you first, may we put you before all things, so we may enjoy the good things around us and the good people among us in the way you have intended. Thank you, Lord, for the witness of your prophets. Thank you, Lord, for the witness of your Word. Amen.

Hymns

The God Of Abraham Praise
Obey My Voice
Here I Am, Lord

Proper 4/Ordinary Time 9
Sunday between May 29 and June 4 inclusive

Second Lesson: Galatians 1:1-12
Theme: Untouched By Human Hands

Call To Worship (Psalm 5:7)

But I, through the abundance of your steadfast love, will enter your house, I will bow down toward your holy temple in awe of you.

Collect

The gift of God is in our midst, a living Word that inspires, revealed directly, proclaimed through the ages, abiding now and forever. Amen.

Prayer Of Confession

This gospel we proclaim, this good news comes from above. It is not the product of a committee or a focus group. It will not conform to our habits or confirm our prejudices. This gospel comes directly from God and calls us to greater discipleship and an endless hope. Let us with God's help live in the light of God's Word and love each other as children of that God.

Hymns

Holy Manna
Good Night And Good Morning
As Saints Of Old

Proper 4/Ordinary Time 9
Sunday between May 29 and June 4 inclusive

Gospel Lesson: Luke 7:1-10
Theme: Unmatched Faith

Call To Worship (Psalm 32:11)

Be glad in the Lord and rejoice, O righteous, and shout for joy, all you upright in heart.

Collect

Now is the time to worship, sisters and brothers in the Lord. This is the day we have been given. Let us use this wisely. Lord of our time, master of our resources, we offer to you this day by our presence, wholeheartedly or grudgingly, these few moments in which we pray you will speak to us, individually in our hearts, and corporately as your people. We will listen to the words that are spoken, to the music that is played, to the lyrics that are sung, to the voices that speak of joys or sorrows, and most of all we will wait for you to speak to us today. Amen.

Prayer Of Confession

Your faith has saved you; go in peace.

Hymns

Majesty
Thy Word
Come, Now Is The Time To Worship

Proper 5/Ordinary Time 10
Sunday between June 5 and June 11 inclusive

First Lesson: 1 Kings 17:8-16 (17-24)
Theme: Your Word Is Truth

Call To Worship

You who drive across town for a bottomless cup of coffee, gather together in the Lord's house for an endless salvation which is given for all people.

Collect

As the widow responded in her poverty to your servant Elijah, giving and receiving, so we as your people come together to give and receive in endless measure. Amen.

Prayer Of Confession

So many times, Lord, we see examples of your boundless love, yet still we hold back, unsure of your bounty. We pray that we might open our arms for your grace, and that we might offer that grace to others. Amen.

Hymns

Showers Of Blessing
Fill My Cup, Lord
Come To The Water

Proper 5/Ordinary Time 10
Sunday between June 5 and June 11 inclusive

Second Lesson: Galatians 1:11-24
Theme: Major League Turn Around

Call To Worship

Hear, God's people — God turned Paul around. God's intent is to turn all around, that he may be praised for the miracle of our lives. Amen.

Collect (Lamentations 3:22-23)

(Unison) The steadfast love of the Lord never ceases, his mercies never come to an end; they are new every morning; great is your faithfulness.

Prayer Of Confession

Spirit of the living God, fall afresh on us. Melt the hardness of our hearts and turn us again to become your faithful, welcoming people. Amen.

Hymns

Great Is Your Faithfulness
Spirit Of The Living God, Fall Afresh On Me
Wonderful Grace Of Jesus

Proper 5/Ordinary Time 10
Sunday between June 5 and June 11 inclusive

Gospel Lesson: Luke 7:11-17
Theme: Believe It Or Not!

Call To Worship (Psalm 43:4)

I will go to the altar of God, to God my exceeding joy; and I will praise you with the harp, O God, my God.

Collect

God, you are our exceeding joy! You have blessed us by your call to outsiders. You have called even us to be your people! Amen.

Prayer Of Confession

We are all one in Christ. We are all one in the risen Lord. We are all one, God's people among all nations. Amen.

Hymns

Awake, My Soul, And With The Sun *(see page 272)*
You Shall Go Out With Joy
Praise The Lord, Sing Hallelujah

Proper 6/Ordinary Time 11
Sunday between June 12 and June 18 inclusive

First Lesson: 1 Kings 21:1-10 (11-14) 15-21a
Theme: Justice Or Just Us?

Call To Worship (based on Galatians 2:15-20)

One: Yet we know that a person is justified not by the works of the law but through faith in Jesus Christ.

All: And we have come to believe in Christ Jesus, so that we might be justified by faith in Christ, and not by doing the works of the law, because no one will be justified by the works of the law.

One: For through the law I died to the law, so that I might live to God. I have been crucified with Christ;

All: and it is no longer I who live, but it is Christ who lives in me. And the life I now live in the flesh I live by faith in the Son of God, who loved me and gave himself for me.

Collect

Listen God's people — the story is not always pleasant, but God calls us to defend and protect those without power in the face of the powers! Through Christ we are strengthened for this great work. Amen.

Prayer Of Confession

Lord, in the face of racial and economic justice we have been content to stand idly by. We are called to defend those who live without justice, to befriend those who are isolated and on the margins, and to stand up to those in power who run roughshod over your people. Strengthen us, like your prophets, so the powers and principalities may truly know you live among us. Amen.

Hymns

Guide My Feet
Pilgrimage Of Faith *(see page 274)*
Blessed Assurance

Proper 6/Ordinary Time 11
Sunday between June 12 and June 18 inclusive

Second Lesson: Galatians 2:15-21
Theme: The Past Through The Present

Call To Worship (Psalm 5)

Give ear to my words, O Lord; give heed to my sighing.

Listen to the sound of my cry, my King and my God, for to you I pray.

O Lord, in the morning you hear my voice; in the morning I plead my case to you, and watch.

For you are not a God who delights in wickedness; evil will not sojourn with you.

The boastful will not stand before your eyes; you hate all evildoers.

You destroy those who speak lies; the Lord abhors the bloodthirsty and deceitful.

But I, through the abundance of your steadfast love, will enter your house, I will bow down toward your holy temple in awe of you.

Lead me, O Lord, in your righteousness because of my enemies; make your way straight before me.

For there is no truth in their mouths; their hearts are destruction; their throats are open graves; they flatter with their tongues.

Make them bear their guilt, O God; let them fall by their own counsels; because of their many transgressions cast them out, for they have rebelled against you.

But let all who take refuge in you rejoice; let them ever sing for joy. Spread your protection over them, so that those who love your name may exult in you.

For you bless the righteous, O Lord; you cover them with favor as with a shield.

Collect

Our boast, Lord, is not in what we have done but in what you have done for us. Amen.

Prayer Of Confession (Galatians 2:19-20)

One: For through the law I died to the law, so that I might live to God. I have been crucified with Christ;

All: and it is no longer I who live, but it is Christ who lives in me. And the life I now live in the flesh I live by faith in the Son of God, who loved me and gave himself for me.

Hymns

My Hope Is Built On Nothing Less
Fairest Lord Jesus
Joy To The World

Proper 6/Ordinary Time 11
Sunday between June 12 and June 18 inclusive

Gospel Lesson: Luke 7:36—8:3
Theme: Credit Where Credit Is Due

Call To Worship

Lord, move in our midst. Let your will be magnified in our lives so that others will be led to Christ. Fill us this day with a sense of urgency, so that your grace, which gifts us life, may fuel our desire to be your people. These things we pray in your name. Amen.

Collect

This day, and every day, Lord, we call to mind your blessings. This day, and with your help every day, we give back to you, in hopes that with your power you may direct and guide our lives for the work of your kingdom. Like the women who supported your ministry and fed your disciples may we support your ministries and feed your children throughout the world. Amen.

Prayer Of Confession

Lord, like the woman who anointed your feet, we offer our best, though the world doesn't always understand. Accept our gifts this morning and hallow them for your work in this world. Amen.

Hymns

To God Be The Glory
Grace Alone
Jesus Calls Us

Proper 7/Ordinary Time 12
Sunday between June 19 and June 25 inclusive

First Lesson: 1 Kings 19:1-4 (5-7) 8-15a
Theme: Take My Life — Please

Call To Worship

Triumph and tragedy and back to the mountaintop again. Life never stands still, and neither does the Spirit of God. Let us bring our cares and woes with us as we gather as God's people, prepared to receive God's truth and to take that truth out into the world.

Collect

We thank you, Lord, for your presence in our woes as well as our joys. Amen.

Prayer Of Confession

It is easy for us to say that we will take up our cross and follow Jesus until it's actually time to do so. We get tired, worn out, discouraged. Lord, you refreshed Elijah when he'd had enough, and he finally heard you in the sound of sheer silence. We pledge to slow our lives down, to live sabbath, not legalistically, but full of grace and truth, that we might create spaces where it is possible to hear you when you choose to speak. We praise you and pledge to follow you. Amen.

Hymns

Spirit Of The Living God
Take My Life And Let It Be
Fill My Cup, Lord

Proper 7/Ordinary Time 12
Sunday between June 19 and June 25 inclusive

Second Lesson: Galatians 3:23-29
Theme: Grow Up

Call To Worship

Praise God for grace. Praise God for the family which is ours to share. Praise God for our place in that family, equal to all others when it comes to God's love.

Collect

In you, Lord Jesus, there is no east or west, no white or black, no male or female, no rich or poor. We come as one in your sight, approved, loved, and eagerly sought after. For this and for all your blessings we thank you. Amen.

Prayer Of Confession

Lord God, you have called us to grow up, to move beyond the laws which hinder the grace which frees us as men and women of all economic and ethnic backgrounds to come together as one in your name. Our artificial divisions have no place in your kingdom. We pledge to forsake the idolatry of racism, the prison of sexism, the monetary chains that bind us and blind us. We thank you for your family, our family, which gathers in your name. Amen.

Hymns

Open My Eyes That I May See
I Know Not Why God's Wondrous Grace
In Christ There Is No East Or West

Proper 7/Ordinary Time 12
Sunday between June 19 and June 25 inclusive

Gospel Lesson: Luke 8:26-39
Theme: Legionnaires

Call To Worship (based on Psalm 22:19-28)

All: But you, O Lord, do not be far away! O my help, come quickly to my aid!

Younger: I will tell of your name to my brothers and sisters; in the midst of the congregation I will praise you:

Older: You who fear the Lord, praise him! Glorify him; stand in awe of him, all you offspring of Israel!

All: For he did not despise or abhor the affliction of the afflicted; he did not hide his face from me, but heard when I cried to him.

Women: From you comes my praise in the great congregation; my vows I will pay before those who fear him.

Men: The poor shall eat and be satisfied; those who seek him shall praise the Lord. May your hearts live forever!

All: All the ends of the earth shall remember and turn to the Lord; and all the families of the nations shall worship before him.

One: For dominion belongs to the Lord, and he rules over the nations.

Collect

Lord, we proclaim your rule in a world that struggles to recognize you. We have seen you act in our midst, and we have this testimony to give — that you, O Lord, take the part of the poor and the afflicted and the oppressed. In our worship today we seek to glorify you and imitate. Fill our hearts with your Spirit. Move among us, and inspire us. Bless us in our gathering and in our going. Amen.

Prayer Of Confession

Lord, our problems are legion. Our concerns, both spoken and unspoken, mount up, and we pray, knowing that you hear our cry and seek to remedy our ills. The joys you offer are limitless, and the salvation you bring is for everyone. Bless us that we might hear and demonstrate action and concern in imitation of your love for us. Hear us. Heal us. Amen.

Hymns

Our God Is An Awesome God
Precious Lord, Take My Hand
What A Friend We Have In Jesus

Proper 8/Ordinary Time 13
Sunday between June 26 and July 2 inclusive

First Lesson: 2 Kings 2:1-2, 6-14
Theme: Take Up The Mantle

Call To Worship

We come together with so much to say, to do, to ask. God knows. Keep silent.
(A time for silent reflection follows)

Collect

In faith we pray that your saints will be revealed among us, that we may praise you all the more as your fire shines brightly in our lives together. Amen.

Prayer Of Confession

Fire, Lord, chariots, Lord, endings and beginnings. Farewell and hello, new prophets taking up your mantle, familiar faces rising to glory. We confess this day that you are God, that wonders can still be seen in our midst, and those you choose to honor should be honored by us! Chariots of fire, lives in your service, glory, glory, glory. Amen.

Hymns

Amazing Grace
All Hail The Power Of Jesus' Name
And Did Those Slaves *(see page 268)*

Proper 8/Ordinary Time 13
Sunday between June 26 and July 2 inclusive

Second Lesson: Galatians 5:1, 13-25
Theme: Fresh Fruit In Season, Dried Fruit For The Journey

Call To Worship

Listen, people of God: The fruit of the Spirit is love, joy, peace, faith, patience, kindness, generosity, faithfulness, gentleness, and self-control.

Collect

In your name we gather, Lord, set free for service, sent forth with the gospel. Amen.

Prayer Of Confession

Lord, we praise you for the freedom you have granted us in Christ. With your help may we break the bonds of our personal prisons and take hold of the life you have promised in Jesus, bearing the fruits of the Spirit, and sharing these with the world. Amen.

Hymns

Gracious Spirit, Dwell With Me
I Am Thine, O Lord
There Are Many Gifts, But The Same Spirit

Proper 8/Ordinary Time 13
Sunday between June 26 and July 2 inclusive

Gospel Lesson: Luke 9:51-62
Theme: Single Minded, Single Purpose

Call To Worship (based on Psalm 16)

One: Protect me, O God, for in you I take refuge.
All: I say to the Lord, "You are my Lord; I have no good apart from you."
One: The Lord is my chosen portion and my cup; you hold my lot.
All: The boundary lines have fallen for me in pleasant places; I have a goodly heritage.
One: I bless the Lord who gives me counsel; in the night also my heart instructs me.
All: I keep the Lord always before me; because he is at my right hand, I shall not be moved.
One: Therefore my heart is glad, and my soul rejoices; my body also rests secure.
All: You show me the path of life. In your presence there is fullness of joy; in your right hand are pleasures forevermore.

Collect

This day, and every day, Lord, we call to mind your blessings. This day, and with your help every day, we give back to you, in hopes that with your power you may direct and guide our gifts for the work of your kingdom. Amen.

Prayer Of Confession

Lord, you told your disciples, "Foxes have holes, and birds of the air have nests; but the Son of Man has nowhere to lay his head." Even though we may consider ourselves poor, though we may struggle with bills, or feel we have been victims of injustice, we know that in comparison to the rest of the world we are wealthy beyond measure. Today help us to hear your call, to recognize our spiritual poverty and material wealth, and our call to praise your name and become your living presence in the world. Amen.

Hymns

Immortal, Invisible
Sweet Are The Promises
Are Ye Able?

Proper 9/Ordinary Time 14
Sunday between July 3 and July 9 inclusive

First Lesson: 2 Kings 5:1-14
Theme: Too Simple For You?

Call To Worship

Listen to God's servants who have come to tell us about the cure. Do not be lulled by apathy or impressed by language. Look at the hearts of God's servants and come together in peace.

Collect

Lord, we thank you that you have confounded the wisdom of the world and have spoken in simplicity, calling us together as your people. Amen.

Prayer Of Confession

Just as Namaan protested that the cure was too easy, so we also complicate your simple gospel of love and salvation, creating barriers to those who seek you, Lord, preventing them from the healing that will come with a full measure of grace. Shame us when we fail to share the joy of your kingdom, and fill our hearts with gladness when we are faithful. Amen.

Hymns

Joy To The World
Jesus Loves Me, This I Know
The B-I-B-L-E

Proper 9/Ordinary Time 14
Sunday between July 3 and July 9 inclusive

Second Lesson: Galatians 6:(1-6) 7-16
Theme: Carry This, Will Ya?

Call To Worship (Psalm 25:1-10)

One: To you, O Lord, I lift up my soul.

All: O my God, in you I trust; do not let me be put to shame; do not let my enemies exult over me.

One: Do not let those who wait for you be put to shame; let them be ashamed who are wantonly treacherous.

All: Make me to know your ways, O Lord; teach me your paths.

One: Lead me in your truth, and teach me, for you are the God of my salvation; for you I wait all day long.

All: Be mindful of your mercy, O Lord, and of your steadfast love, for they have been from of old.

One: Do not remember the sins of my youth or my transgressions; according to your steadfast love remember me, for your goodness' sake, O Lord!

All: Good and upright is the Lord; therefore he instructs sinners in the way.

One: He leads the humble in what is right, and teaches the humble his way.

All: All the paths of the Lord are steadfast love and faithfulness, for those who keep his covenant and his decrees.

Collect

God of history, God of the world, we put our trust in you. Lead us in your truth. Let the light of your Word and the comfort of your Spirit, along with the wisdom of your Spirit, be our guide in our path as your people. Amen.

Prayer Of Confession

Lord of gifts, you have called us to love you with our soul, our strength, our mind, and our heart. We acknowledge your gifts to us, and we return them with thanks to your service. Amen.

Hymns

In The Cross Of Christ I Glory
Gracious Spirit, Dwell With Me
I Am Thine, O Lord

Proper 9/Ordinary Time 14
Sunday between July 3 and July 9 inclusive

Gospel Lesson: Luke 10:1-11, 16-20
Theme: You Ain't Seen Nothing Yet

Call To Worship (Psalm 66:1-9)

Make a joyful noise to God, all the earth; sing the glory of his name; give to him glorious praise.

Say to God, "How awesome are your deeds! Because of your great power, your enemies cringe before you.

All the earth worships you; they sing praises to you, sing praises to your name." *Selah*

Come and see what God has done: he is awesome in his deeds among mortals.

He turned the sea into dry land; they passed through the river on foot. There we rejoiced in him,

who rules by his might forever, whose eyes keep watch on the nations — let the rebellious not exalt themselves. *Selah*

Bless our God, O peoples, let the sound of his praise be heard, who has kept us among the living, and has not let our feet slip.

Collect

One: The Lord sends us out like lambs among wolves — let us not act as wolves among God's lambs, but in gathering together recognize the mission and ministry we share.

All: The Spirit of God has come near unto us! God, we thank you for this Spirit and pray that you will inspire us to take risks for the kingdom. Amen.

Prayer Of Confession

Jesus, Lord, you told us you saw Satan fall like lightning. Cast out the false spirit of fear among us and renew your spirit of truth. Amen.

Hymns

Come, Now Is The Time To Worship
Spirit Of The Living God
You Shall Go Out With Joy

Proper 10/Ordinary Time 15
Sunday between July 10 and July 16 inclusive

First Lesson: Amos 7:7-17
Theme: Got A Life

Call To Worship

One: Lord we come before you with cares and worries.
All: We are worried and distracted by many things.
One: Today we ask that you guide us in our worship.
All: Help us to choose the better part,
One: to sit at your feet Lord,
All: and to hear your holy word.

Collect

Lord, clear our minds, calm our hearts, focus our wills upon the presence of your Spirit in our midst. We desire to see Christ in your written word, in the words from the pulpit, in the sound of our shared music, and in the voices of our sisters and brothers of all ages in our midst. These things we pray in the name of the risen Christ. Amen.

Prayer Of Confession

God of glory, too long have we hidden ourselves from your light, afraid we might truly become disciples. We have clung to our false gods of security and fear, turning away from the cross because of the wisdom of this world. Today we intend to face your light, and are resolved that we will either be dissolved by your power or transformed by your love into real disciples of Jesus Christ. Great God of glory, preserve us, remold us, make us your people with your followers around the world. Amen.

Hymns

O Day Of Rest And Gladness
Will You Let Me Be Your Servant?
I Know Not Why God's Wondrous Grace

Proper 10/Ordinary Time 15
Sunday between July 10 and July 16 inclusive

Second Lesson: Colossians 1:1-14
Theme: Victory Parade

Call To Worship (based on Colossians 1:9)

One: For this reason, since the day we heard it, we have not ceased praying for you and asking that you may be filled with the knowledge of God's will in all spiritual wisdom and understanding,

All: so that we may lead lives worthy of the Lord, fully pleasing to him, as we bear fruit in every good work and as we grow in the knowledge of God.

Collect

In your light we see the world revealed as your own, and we as your servants. As we name you Savior and Lord, claim us please as your servants. Amen.

Prayer Of Confession (Colossians 1:15-23)

Christ is the image of the invisible God, the firstborn of all creation; for in him all things in heaven and on earth were created, things visible and invisible, whether thrones or dominions or rulers or powers — all things have been created through him and for him.

He himself is before all things, and in him all things hold together.

He is the head of the body, the church; he is the beginning, the firstborn from the dead, so that he might come to have first place in everything.

For in him all the fullness of God was pleased to dwell, and through him God was pleased to reconcile to himself all things, whether on earth or in heaven, by making peace through the blood of his cross.

And you who were once estranged and hostile in mind, doing evil deeds, he has now reconciled in his fleshly body through death, so as to present you holy and blameless and irreproachable before him — provided that you continue securely established and steadfast in the faith, without shifting from the hope promised by the gospel that you heard, which has been proclaimed to every creature under heaven.

Hymns

A Wonderful Savior Is Jesus Our Lord
Alas! And Did My Savior Bleed
God Of Grace And God Of Glory

Proper 10/Ordinary Time 15
Sunday between July 10 and July 16 inclusive

Gospel Lesson: Luke 10:25-37
Theme: Question And Answer

Call To Worship

The question has been asked for us — the answer is more graphic than we allow ourselves to hear. Who is our neighbor? You know. I know. We know.

Collect (based on Luke 10:25, 27)

Right Side: What must we do to inherit eternal life?
Left Side: We shall love the Lord your God with all our heart, and with all our soul, and with all our strength, and with all our mind; and our neighbor as ourselves.

Prayer Of Confession

We thank you, Heavenly Father, for this family of faith. We thank you for willing ears to hear, hands to work, hearts to love. Fill us with your Spirit as we call to mind the words of your Son and our Savior, saying in one voice: Our Father, who art in heaven, hallowed be thy name. Thy kingdom come. Thy will be done on earth as it is in heaven. Give us this day our daily bread. Forgive us our debts as we forgive our debtors. And lead us not into temptation, but deliver us from evil. For thine is the kingdom, the power, and the glory forever. Amen.

Hymns

In The Rifted Rock I'm Resting
Shine, Jesus, Shine
If All You Want

Proper 11/Ordinary Time 16
Sunday between July 17 and July 23 inclusive

First Lesson: Amos 8:1-12
Theme: Bad Pun, Bad News

Call To Worship (Psalm 99)

One: The Lord is king; let the peoples tremble! He sits enthroned upon the cherubim; let the earth quake!

All: The Lord is great in Zion; he is exalted over all the peoples.

One: Let them praise your great and awesome name. Holy is he!

All: Mighty King, lover of justice, you have established equity; you have executed justice and righteousness in Jacob.

One: Extol the Lord our God; worship at his footstool. Holy is he!

All: Moses and Aaron were among his priests, Samuel also was among those who called on his name. They cried to the Lord, and he answered them.

One: He spoke to them in the pillar of cloud; they kept his decrees, and the statutes that he gave them.

All: O Lord our God, you answered them; you were a forgiving God to them, but an avenger of their wrongdoings.

One And All: Extol the Lord our God, and worship at his holy mountain; for the Lord our God is holy.

Collect

Lord, we praise your name, and humbly beg your presence in our midst as we listen to the challenging words of your prophet! Amen.

Prayer Of Confession

May we heed your warning, Lord, before it is too late, that we might serve you not in word but with our hearts, with our hands, with our lives. Amen.

Hymns

In Thy Holy Place We Bow
For the Fruit Of All Creation
Lift Every Voice And Sing

Proper 11/Ordinary Time 16
Sunday between July 17 and July 23 inclusive

Second Lesson: Colossians 1:15-28
Theme: Second Verse, Same As The First

Call To Worship (Colossians 1:15-16)

(Unison) [Jesus] is the image of the invisible God, the firstborn of all creation; for in him all things in heaven and on earth were created, things visible and invisible, whether thrones or dominions or rulers or powers — all things have been created through him and for him.

Collect

Let us continue in faith, people of God, that we will not have run this race in vain. Let us rejoice in our sufferings, and in God's triumph!

Prayer Of Confession (Galatians 6:9-10)

So let us not grow weary in doing what is right, for we will reap at harvest-time, if we do not give up. So then, whenever we have an opportunity, let us work for the good of all, and especially for those of the family of faith.

Hymns

Great Is The Lord!
Guide My Feet, While I Run This Race
Glorious Things Of Thee Are Spoken

Proper 11/Ordinary Time 16
Sunday between July 17 and July 23 inclusive

Gospel Lesson: Luke 10:38-42
Theme: Not You Two, Again!

Call To Worship

Peace to this house! Like the home of Mary and Martha, there is conflict and disagreement, but there is also love, and there is Jesus. Peace to this house! Come!

Collect (2 Corinthians 8:12-14)

One: For if the eagerness is there, the gift is acceptable according to what one has — not according to what one does not have.

All: I do not mean that there should be relief for others and pressure on you, but it is a question of a fair balance between your present abundance and their need, so that their abundance may be for your need, in order that there may be a fair balance.

Prayer Of Confession (Exodus 24:7)

"All that the Lord has spoken we will do, and we will be obedient."

Hymns

Come, Now Is The Time For Worship
Praise, I Will Praise You, Lord
In The Garden

Proper 12/Ordinary Time 17
Sunday between July 24 and July 30 inclusive

First Lesson: Hosea 1:2-10
Theme: Children Of The Living God

Call To Worship

Though we have been no people, we are now God's people. Let us gather in God's name to praise him, to adore him, to worship him.

Collect

There is no place so strange, no distance so far, no sin so great, that you will not find us and gather us again as your people. For this we praise you, forgiving God. Amen.

Prayer Of Confession

For every time we have felt distant from you, through our own sins and the sins of the world, we know that you have waited for us to turn and return. We confess our sins. Forgive us. Give us your guidance. Amen.

Hymns

All Hail The Power Of Jesus' Name (Diadem)
Spirit Of The Living God
Blessed Assurance

Proper 12/Ordinary Time 17
Sunday between July 24 and July 30 inclusive

Second Lesson: Colossians 2:6-15 (16-19)
Theme: Debt Relief

Call To Worship (based on Colossians 2:6-10)

One: As you therefore have received Christ Jesus the Lord, continue to live your lives in him,

All: ... rooted and built up in him and established in the faith, just as you were taught, abounding in thanksgiving.

One: See to it that no one takes you captive through philosophy and empty deceit, according to human tradition, according to the elemental spirits of the universe, and not according to Christ.

All: For in him the whole fullness of deity dwells bodily, and you have come to fullness in him, who is the head of every ruler and authority.

Collect

We gather, Lord, in gratitude for your boundless forgiveness and your will to transform us in glory. Amen.

Prayer Of Confession

Heavenly Father, we acknowledge that you are the source of the faith that we share. It is your gift to us, and not our own creation. You are the author of all that lives and moves and breathes. Today we come together to proclaim that Jesus Christ is Lord. We gather together not because of shared interests or social standing but because we are one body in Christ. Bind our hearts together in this purpose, that we might praise your name and call others into this body. We bless your holy name. Amen.

Hymns

Praise To The Lord, The Almighty
Christian Let Your Burning Light
Come, Come Ye Saints

Proper 12/Ordinary Time 17
Sunday between July 24 and July 30 inclusive

Gospel Lesson: Luke 11:1-13
Theme: Our Father With A Twist

Call To Worship

We as your people are privileged, O Lord. As we accept the gift of your living Word may we given back to you in small measure what you have given us beyond measure. Accept our presence here and inspire us to be your witnesses in your world. Amen.

Collect (Luke 11:2-4)

Father, hallowed be your name.

Your kingdom come.

Give us each day our daily bread.

And forgive us our sins, for we ourselves forgive everyone indebted to us. And do not bring us to the time of trial.

Amen.

Prayer Of Confession

Lord, you are better than us. We come through when we have to. Why don't we give you credit, Heavenly Father, for your endless love and concern? We confess that we would limit your bounty to our selected few. Push us to widen the circle of our fellowship, and to actively seek those who are far off, that they might be brought near, into your family. Amen.

Hymns

Great Is Thy Faithfulness
Holy Spirit, Come With Power
My Hope Is Built On Nothing Less

Proper 13/Ordinary Time 18
Sunday between July 31 and August 6 inclusive

First Lesson: Hosea 11:1-11
Theme: All My Compassion Is Aroused

Call To Worship

One: Blessed be God, who confers the task of ministry on each of us.

All: Blessed be God, who confers the task of ministry on all of us.

One: Let us gladly accept the gift of ministry which is ours.

All: Let us even more gladly accept the gift of this church, as we jointly share in worship, praise, prayer, and the ministry of the eternal gospel.

Collect

We knew, God of compassion, that you would never forget us. We praise you in your waiting patiently for our repentance and return to you. Amen.

Prayer Of Confession

Lord, help us to hear more than the words spoken by our sisters and brothers, their concerns and joys shared aloud. Help us to look into our hearts for those concerns and joys too deep for words. We lift in prayer this morning all caregivers and those for whom they care. We remember those who bear a great burden of physical or emotional pain. We call to mind those whose suffering is mental. We recall the ones who have left this life behind, as well as those who may still mourn for them. We celebrate with those who have experienced joy. We laugh with those who rejoice, and sing with those moved by the Spirit. Bless us as we seek to share each other's burdens and pray each other's prayers. Amen.

Hymns

This Is My Father's World
Who Is Like God?
Great Is Your Faithfulness

Proper 13/Ordinary Time 18
Sunday between July 31 and August 6 inclusive

Second Lesson: Colossians 3:1-11
Theme: Reading Our Own Obituary

Call To Worship

One: Come, let us gather to worship our God.
All: Let us rejoice for this hour of praise.
One: Let us resolve to become God's people.
All: Let us rely on God's strength to accomplish this purpose.
One: Hear, O God's people, the Lord our God, the Lord is one.
All: With all our heart and all our soul and all our strength and all our mind we love the Lord.
One: Hear, O God's people, the Lord our God, the Lord is one.
All: As we trust in God, so we pledge to love our neighbors as ourselves.
One: Let us pray.

Collect

Lord, the world around us is constantly changing. The fashion of one year is gone the next. The concerns of one season are forgotten with a change in time. The only delight which never fails comes from our love for you and for each other, and in our study of your holy word. Hear our prayer this day, as we seek to magnify your holy name, that at the name of Jesus, every knee should bow. This will come to pass, your perfect will made manifest on earth as it is in heaven, in a time of your choosing. As we wait for that glorious day we shed our daily cares so we may come together in this sweet hour of prayer and praise. Amen.

Prayer Of Confession

God of sacrifice, patient and loving Lord, we have learned again what we have always known — that to die to this life is to live forever, that to lose the things of this fading world is to gain everything, that to reject vanity is to gain substance. Bless us as we pledge to remember once more what you have striven to remind us always. Amen.

Hymns

Sweet Hour Of Prayer
When I Survey The Wondrous Cross (alternate tune)
Precious Lord, Take My Hand

Proper 13/Ordinary Time 18
Sunday between July 31 and August 6 inclusive

Gospel Lesson: Luke 12:13-21
Theme: Wise Fool

Call To Worship

As we gather together let us be on guard against all kinds of greed, for life does not consist of an abundance of possessions.

Collect

God, we confess that we have stored up the wealth of our nation while our sisters and brothers around the world go without. We pray for the strength to throw caution, safety, and prudence to the wind, so we might trust you to provide for our future as we empty our store-houses for the benefit of those in your family who have nothing. Amen.

Prayer Of Confession (based on Luke 12:15)

Father, we call to mind the words of your Son, when he said, "Take care! Be on your guard against all kinds of greed; for one's life does not consist in the abundance of possessions." We are tempted to ground ourselves in our possessions and the relentless pursuit of more. Turn our hearts toward the joy of your kingdom as we give back to you a measure of what we hold in stewardship for this short time. Let our lives become an offering of our love in addition to our gifts of our material goods. Thank you, Lord of all, for this time of worship. Amen.

Hymns

Holy, Holy, Holy
Immortal, Invisible
Praise, I Will Praise You Lord

Proper 14/Ordinary Time 19
Sunday between August 7 and August 13 inclusive

First Lesson: Isaiah 1:1, 10-20
Theme: Seek Justice, Defend The Cause

Call To Worship

One: We call the hour of prayer sweet in our songs,
All: but our prayer is often a call for comfort.
Right Side: If you choose to comfort us in our prayers this morning,
Left Side: let it be the comfort that comes from knowing we are needed.
Upstairs: Let the prophet be heard in our midst.
Downstairs: Let the Word of God be heard personally.
All: Here in this place, let our prayers rise, let your challenge descend. Move in our midst, O Spirit of God.

Collect

Here we are, Lord, once more finding ourselves at the beginning of new life, new hope, new possibilities. Help us to shed the constraints of the past to take hold of the prophetic vision you have set before us. Amen.

Prayer Of Confession

Lord, these are our petitions this day. We have confessed our sins, shared our sorrows, and celebrated our joys. Hear both that which was spoken and this, which is silently lifted up to you. We praise you, O God, and thank you for the community of faith you have shared with us. Amen.

Hymns

Sanctuary
Here In This Place
Lift Every Voice And Sing

Proper 14/Ordinary Time 19
Sunday between August 7 and August 13 inclusive

Second Lesson: Hebrews 11:1-3, 8-16
Theme: I'm That Certain

Call To Worship

The wind encircles and envelopes all
Of life and yet unseen we see when past
The splintered trunks and limbs of those that fall
Or far afield those the storm has cast.

The Spirit from the womb and long before
Has tumbling wrenched our hopes and dreams from view
So homeless but not hopeless by the sea
We seek new shores when God makes all things new.

The Spirit, like the wind, will strong endure,
For both are solid, not like legend's wraith.
So if they are not seen we can be sure
Of God's existence. We depend on faith.

This substance of things hoped for can be won
When faith and hope with love in us are one.

Collect

God, you have given us examples, not only in scripture, but among the sisters and brothers who share this fellowship with us! We thank you and praise you for this gift. Amen.

Prayer Of Confession

We have so many examples, Lord, that we cannot complain about the task you set before us, but following those who have gone before we aim to set out in mission and ministry to your hurting world. Amen.

Hymns

We Walk By Faith And Not By Sight
Doxology
This Is The Threefold Faith

Proper 14/Ordinary Time 19
Sunday between August 7 and August 13 inclusive

Gospel Lesson: Luke 12:32-40
Theme: Finding Your Heart

Call To Worship (based on Psalm 33:13-22)

One:	The Lord looks down from heaven; he sees all humankind.
All:	From where he sits enthroned he watches all the inhabitants of the earth —
Left Side:	he who fashions the hearts of them all, and observes all their deeds.
Right Side:	Truly the eye of the Lord is on those who fear him, on those who hope in his steadfast love,
Women:	our soul waits for the Lord; he is our help and shield.
Men:	Our heart is glad in him, because we trust in his holy name.
Old And Young:	Let your steadfast love, O Lord, be upon us, even as we hope in you.
One:	Let us pray.

Collect

Great Lord of all, we gather together to ask your blessing. You have watched us in our travels, in our coming and in our going out, and in our returning. You have seen us, and have loved us, and love us still. Let your Spirit dwell among us in our worshiping today, and in our going out again to perform your will. We praise you, we raise our prayers, we sing in your honor. Bless us in all we do. Amen.

Prayer Of Confession (based on Luke 12:34)

Where our treasure is, there our heart will be also. What treasure can we have outside of you? Amen.

Hymns

If All You Want
Dona Nobis Pacem
God Be With You Till We Meet Again

Proper 15/Ordinary Time 20
Sunday between August 14 and August 20 inclusive

First Lesson: Isaiah 5:1-7
Theme: Shopping In The Grape Aisle

Call To Worship

Our lives are orchards, bearing fruit according to our will and God's grace. As the vine opens her leaves to receive the nourishment of the sun, so let us open our hearts to receive the blessed nourishment from God's Son.

Collect (based on Psalm 82)

Lord of judgment, you have asked us to give justice to the weak and the orphan, to maintain the right of the lowly, to rescue the weak and the needy, and to deliver them from the hand of the wicked. Too often we have used your church as a place to shelter ourselves from your call, rather than to be challenged by it. Today we ask you to rise up, O God. The nations belong to you. Judge the earth. Cause your righteousness to live among us. Heal us. Help us in this ministry you have shared with us. Amen.

Prayer Of Confession

One: This is your word for today. Your vision sharply challenges us. The needs are great. Our efforts must match your commitment and ever-present faithfulness. Bless us in our time of giving and receiving.

All: Let us run with perseverance the race that is set before us.

Hymns

I Sing The Mighty Power Of God
Lord, With Devotion We Pray
Spirit Of God! Descend

Proper 15/Ordinary Time 20
Sunday between August 14 and August 20 inclusive

Second Lesson: Hebrews 11:29—12:2
Theme: Fixing Our Eyes On Jesus

Call To Worship

Come, God's people, come to worship and adore the Lord of our lives, the planner of each day. Offer up your fears and give them over to the God who created sun and moon and stars. Call to mind again not only your commitment to God's kingdom but your pledge to work for it as well.

Collect

We praise your name for the cloud of witnesses who serve as an example to us, both those who have gone before and those who live in our midst. Help us, we pray, to praise, love, and serve you not only as individuals, but as a body of believers who trust in your Word. These things we pray in your mighty name. Amen.

Prayer Of Confession

God of our days, we have journeyed long as your people and there is still far to go. Real and imagined fears surround us. May we never lose sight of you. We are surrounded by a cloud of witnesses, yet sometimes we simply feel surrounded by clouds. Guide us, guard us, inspire us, and send us forth as your people to be witnesses to Jesus and the way of Jesus. These things we pray as your people, as your disciples. Amen.

Hymns

Come, Now Is The Time To Worship
I Know Not Why God's Wondrous Grace
Guide My Feet, While I Run This Race

Proper 15/Ordinary Time 20
Sunday between August 14 and August 20 inclusive

Gospel Lesson: Luke 12:49-56
Theme: The Real Weather Channel

Call To Worship

One: The worlds were prepared by the Word of God.
All: Follow God with courage!

Collect

God's people, we have been blessed with God's Word. But even if we were not so blessed, we could still find our way with God's wind in our face by day and God's story told in the majesty of the heavens by night. Come, God is great. Let us tell God.

Prayer Of Confession

How many ways do you have to tell us, God, that your kingdom is always near and the return of your Son always soon? We wait no longer for you to batter our hearts. We confess you are Creator, Redeemer, and Lord. Amen.

Hymns

How Great Thou Art
No Night There
Soon And Very Soon

Proper 16/Ordinary Time 21
Sunday between August 21 and August 27 inclusive

First Lesson: Jeremiah 1:4-10
Theme: Too Many Excuses

Call To Worship (based on Psalm 71)

One: In God we have always taken refuge and have never been put to shame.

All: God will rescue us in righteousness. God is a refuge always available to us.

One: Hear us, God, and deliver us once more. You have always been our hope.

All: From birth and before we have relied on you, Lord. Our mouths are filled with your praise.

One And All: We will ever praise you!

Collect

Appoint us, Lord, your prophetic people, that we might speak to the powers of this world your message of repentance and hope. Amen.

Prayer Of Confession

Too young, too old, too busy, not ready, too able, not able — Heavenly Father we are full of excuses. Yet you are Lord, Creator, Redeemer, who has remembered us in all ages. As your people we ask that you send us those who need your Word, for you have promised to be with us, even to the end of the age! Amen.

Hymns

In The Rifted Rock I'm Resting
Lord, Listen To Your Children Praying
Go, My Children

Proper 16/Ordinary Time 21
Sunday between August 21 and August 27 inclusive

Second Lesson: Hebrews 12:18-29
Theme: This Is Doable!

Call To Worship

(Unison) The world is full of things we fear, of terrors that threaten to engulf us, of obstacles we cannot ignore — but we are called to the city of the living God, where the Lamb who bears the marks of slaughter bids us peace and welcomes us forever to sing before the throne. We can do this. Let us worship our God today.

Collect

Gentle shepherd, in quietness you speak louder than the thunder of Mount Sinai. We listen.

(Silence for ten seconds)

We hear. Amen.

Prayer Of Confession

We quailed in the desert, we who were called out of slavery, because the storm on the mountain frightened us. Now we cower because the Prince of Peace calls us to live a life worthy of the calling, conforming to the commands of God's kingdom and not the dictates of an insane world. Let us approach with the knowledge that if we cannot come forward to claim Jesus, we have no refuge left when the storms of life finally rage about us. Amen.

Hymns

Majesty
Gentle Shepherd
When The Storms Of Life Are Raging, Stand By Me

Proper 16/Ordinary Time 21
Sunday between August 21 and August 27 inclusive

Gospel Lesson: Luke 13:10-17
Theme: Joy In Healing

Call To Worship (Psalm 71:1-6)

One: In you, O Lord, I take refuge; let me never be put to shame.

All: In your righteousness deliver me and rescue me; incline your ear to me and save me.

One: Be to me a rock of refuge, a strong fortress, to save me, for you are my rock and my fortress.

All: Rescue me, O my God, from the hand of the wicked, from the grasp of the unjust and cruel.

One: For you, O Lord, are my hope, my trust, O Lord, from my youth.

All: Upon you I have leaned from my birth; it was you who took me from my mother's womb. My praise is continually of you.

Collect

Lord of love, you are our refuge and our strength, a present help in times of trouble. This day we pray for your light to shine in our midst as we gather together as your people. In good times and in bad times we pray for the strength to tell your wonderful deeds throughout the earth. You are our hope; we are your children. Together we praise your name. Amen.

Prayer Of Confession

Lord, we are blessed with this marvelous fellowship which you have found for us. We thank you for planting us in the midst of the people of God. Hear our petitions, and grant our earnest prayers. Bless us in our celebrations. Today we share each other's woes, joys, failures, and triumphs. We know there is nothing we shall encounter that we cannot endure with your presence and help. Thank you, Lord. Amen.

Hymns

Praise To The Lord, The Almighty

Just As I Am

A Hymn For Anointing (vv. 1 & 2) *(see page 267)*

Proper 17/Ordinary Time 22
Sunday between August 28 and September 3 inclusive

First Lesson: Jeremiah 2:4-13
Theme: Memory Aid

Call To Worship

One: Great is the Lord.
All: Great is the Lord that is revealed to us in the Word.
One: Great is the Lord.
All: Great is the Lord that is revealed to us in the world.

Collect (built around Deuteronomy 6:6-9, The Message)

Children: How can we remember the Word of God so we do not stray?
All: What shall we do so we and our children always remember God's goodness?
One: Write these commandments that I've given you today on your hearts. Get them inside of you and then get them inside your children.
All: Talk about them wherever you are, sitting at home or walking in the street; talk about them from the time you get up in the morning until you fall into bed at night.
One: Tie them on your hands and foreheads as a reminder;
All: inscribe them on the doorposts of your homes and on your city gates.

Prayer Of Confession

God of glory, how is it that we could follow idols when you have offered us the living water and the bread of life? We shall strive to hold your Word in our hearts that we might never again forget. Amen.

Hymns

Great Is The Lord
Heart With Loving Heart United
Shall We Gather At The River?

Proper 17/Ordinary Time 22
Sunday between August 28 and September 3 inclusive

Second Lesson: Hebrews 13:1-8, 15-16
Theme: Just A Brief Word, Please

Call To Worship (Hebrews 13:1-2)

One: Let mutual love continue.

All: Do not neglect to show hospitality to strangers, for through their hospitality, some have entertained angels without knowing it.

Collect

Lord of all creation, holy and just, the source of all good, the protector of the oppressed, we come before you this morning intent upon praising you, and raising up our voices in song and word. Lift up our hearts within us, that we may go forth to witness to your love and power. These things we pray in your name. Amen.

Prayer Of Confession

All: The Lord make his face to shine upon you, and be gracious to you; the Lord lift up his countenance upon you,

Children: and give you peace.

Hymns

It Is Well With My Soul
For We Are Strangers No More
Brothers And Sisters Of Mine Are The Hungry

Proper 17/Ordinary Time 22
Sunday between August 28 and September 3 inclusive

Gospel Lesson: Luke 14:1, 7-14
Theme: First, Last, And Always

Call To Worship

God has put into our hands the blessings of this fellowship, and into our care the needs of this world. Let us come together in praise and thanksgiving for God's love and trust in us.

Collect

Lord, we thank you for the blessings of your Holy Word, and for the inspiration of your Holy Spirit. We come to receive, not that we should hold these blessings within ourselves, but that we might go forth into the world to share this good news. Even as we sit here, we think of excuses, great God, of why others will have to carry this Word. We pray that you will sweep away our fears and send us forward, renewed and restored, ready to be your witnessing people. These things we pray, trusting in you. Amen.

Prayer Of Confession

These gifts we bring, precious Lord, are what we feel we can spare. These gifts we bring, gracious Lord, were yours from the beginning, on loan to us. These gifts we bring, mighty Lord, should accomplish great things, with your aid. Instill in us your Spirit, which is ever giving to us. Amen.

Hymns

What Is This Place?
A Wonderful Savior Is Jesus My Lord
I Know That My Redeemer Lives

Proper 18/Ordinary Time 23
Sunday between September 4 and September 10 inclusive

First Lesson: Jeremiah 18:1-11
Theme: Pottery Lesson

Call To Worship

Come, let us walk to the shop of the heavenly potter, and observe in each other your perfect handiwork.

Collect

Lord, we thank you today for your goodness. We offer in return what seems good to us. Accept our lives and use us for your work in the world. We pray this in the name of Jesus Christ. Amen.

Prayer Of Confession (based on 2 Corinthians 7:4ff)

Heavenly Father, what a treasure we have in the clay jars of our lives, molded by you, shaped by your love, to be useful vessels for your Holy Spirit. We thank you for the blessings of the ministry that we share, and confess you as Potter, Shaper, Redeemer. Amen.

Hymns

O Worship The Lord
Have Thine Own Way
God Be With You

Proper 18/Ordinary Time 23
Sunday between September 4 and September 10 inclusive

Second Lesson: Philemon 1-21
Theme: Refresh My Guts In Christ

Call To Worship (based on Deuteronomy 30:15-16)

One: God has set before us today life and prosperity, death and adversity.

All: Let us obey the commandments of the Lord our God by loving the Lord our God, walking in his ways, and observing his commandments.

Collect

Great God of glory, we come together today not only to praise, but to pray for transformation. May your gospel consume us, that we might live to spread the word about the salvation offered to all. Amen.

Prayer Of Confession

Lord, we have worshiped the false idol of racism. We have discriminated between others and ourselves, recognizing distinctions of race, economics, ethnicity, and failing to recognize each other as your children. Refresh us as we renounce the slavery of our false gods and seek the freedom of Christ in our lives. Amen.

Hymns

Jesus Loves Me
O Master Let Me Walk With Thee
Comfort, Comfort, O My People

Proper 18/Ordinary Time 23
Sunday between September 4 and September 10 inclusive

Gospel Lesson: Luke 14:25-33
Theme: Hiring The Right Architect

Call To Worship (Psalm 126)

One: When the Lord restored the fortunes of Zion, we were like those who dream.

All: Then our mouth was filled with laughter, and our tongue with shouts of joy; then it was said among the nations, "The Lord has done great things for them."

Left Side: The Lord has done great things for us, and we rejoiced.

Right Side: Restore our fortunes, O Lord, like the watercourses in the Negeb.

Upstairs: May those who sow in tears reap with shouts of joy.

Downstairs: Those who go out weeping, bearing the seed for sowing, shall come home with shouts of joy, carrying their sheaves.

Collect

Our lives surrendered, then returned in full,
We count the cost and then become God's will.

Prayer Of Confession

Lord, we have counted the cost, we have laid a foundation, we have prepared for your great harvest. We are assembled here as willing workers. We state before this community of faith that we are ready. You have done great things for us, and we have rejoiced. You have restored our fortunes. Now challenge us, Lord, to reap with shouts of joy, the harvest of souls, the friendless, the hungry, the hated, the forgotten, your many children young and old who are starved for your kingdom. There are enough of us for this work, if we dedicate our lives in your service. We love you, Lord. We pray for your strength. Amen.

Hymns

Come, O Creator Spirit, Come
Count Well The Cost *(see page 276)*
Take Up Your Cross

Proper 19/Ordinary Time 24
Sunday between September 11 and September 17 inclusive

First Lesson: Jeremiah 4:11-12, 22-28
Theme: Disaster!

Call To Worship

One: Come, let us worship the Lord our God.
All: Come, let us worship the creator of all things.
Women: Let all who hear us praise God's magnificent name.
Men: Let all who cannot hear us know through your saving mercy, your glory and majesty.
All: Let all creation join in praise of our God.
One: Let us pray together.

Collect

Lord, you have given us this day and this day only. You have granted us this hour, this moment, to imitate your boundless giving in our own more limited way. Bless us in this time of prayer and worship, and help us rededicate ourselves to your service as your servants. Amen.

Prayer Of Confession (based on Psalm 51)

Create in us a new heart, O Lord, and put a new right spirit within us. You know our weaknesses. You know our faults. Yet you love us and call us to your service. In this hour of worship we celebrate your faithfulness and seek to reply with our own faithfulness. Let us hear joy and gladness. Forgive us our sins. Hear our prayers and petitions. Bless us in our gathering today. We pray these things in the name of Jesus Christ. Amen.

Hymns

Give Thanks With A Thankful Heart
Thy Word
Softly And Tenderly Jesus Is Calling

Proper 19/Ordinary Time 24
Sunday between September 11 and September 17 inclusive

Second Lesson: 1 Timothy 1:12-17
Theme: Immortal, Invisible

Call To Worship (based on 1 Timothy 1:15)

Here is a saying you can count on, so listen God's people! Jesus came to save the lost. That's me and you, our neighbors, and our friends halfway around the world whose love we will enjoy through all of eternity. Let us gather together in God's love.

Collect

Immortal, invisible, eternal king, the only God, to you be honor and glory and power. We praise you, from whom all blessings flow!

Prayer Of Confession

(A time of silence)
Even Paul.
(A time of silence)
Even me.
(A time of silence)
All of us.
(A time of silence)
Amen.

Hymns

Awake, My Soul, And With The Sun (Doxology Album Version — *see page* 272)
Immortal, Invisible
Marvelous Grace Of Our Loving Lord

Proper 19/Ordinary Time 24
Sunday between September 11 and September 17 inclusive

Gospel Lesson: Luke 15:1-10
Theme: Looking To Find

Call To Worship

Rejoice with me, God's people. The lost has been found!

Collect

Bright and shiny are the coins when we find them, no matter how dull and scraped when we lost them. Lord, you make all things new, especially our lives. Renew us, revive us, restore us. Find us. Amen.

Prayer Of Confession

Rejoice with us! The lost sheep has been found! The lost coin has been recovered! Lost lives can be saved. We cannot find if we don't look. We cannot save if we don't seek. As God's people we renew our resolve to serve those who are lost to God and society now and toward the next world. Amen.

Hymns

Revive Us Again
Sanctuary
Amazing Grace

Proper 20/Ordinary Time 25
Sunday between September 18 and September 24 inclusive

First Lesson: Jeremiah 8:18—9:1
Theme: Real Relief

Call To Worship (based on Psalm 113)

Women: Praise the Lord! Praise, O servants of the Lord; praise the name of the Lord.

Men: Blessed be the name of the Lord from this time on and forevermore.

Right Side: From the rising of the sun to its setting the name of the Lord is to be praised.

Left Side: The Lord is high above all nations, and his glory above the heavens.

Women: Who is like the Lord our God, who is seated on high,

Men: who looks far down on the heavens and the earth?

Right Side: He raises the poor from the dust, and lifts the needy from the ash heap,

Left Side: to make them sit with princes, with the princes of his people.

All: Praise the Lord!

Collect (built around Jeremiah 8:20-22)

One: "The harvest is past, the summer is ended, and we are not saved."

All: For the hurt of my poor people I am hurt, I mourn, and dismay has taken hold of me.

One And All: Is there no balm in Gilead? Is there no physician there? Why then has the health of my poor people not been restored?

Hear our prayer, Lord, as we call to you from the depths of our misery. Hear our prayer as we realize we are called to minister to the misery of others. Bless us in our brokenness with your balm, with your peace that passes understanding. Find us. Heal us. Amen.

Prayer Of Confession

Lord, we will praise, on this day and every day. We have seen the terrible power of evil in the world, but we have felt, in our hearts, your indomitable spirit of love, and know you will triumph. We take our stand, this day, with you, on the side of the poor and the needy. We take our place with the marginalized, the hungry, the terrified, the lonely. We pray that you will call us in ministry to your people everywhere, as surely as you have called us into your presence here in this church today. Be with us. Sustain us. Abide with us. We praise you! Praise the Lord! Amen.

Hymns

Balm In Gilead
O Healing River
Whom Shall I Send?

Proper 20/Ordinary Time 25
Sunday between September 18 and September 24 inclusive

Second Lesson: 1 Timothy 2:1-7
Theme: Pray For Who?

Call To Worship (Psalm 113:1-4)

One: Praise the Lord! Praise, O servants of the Lord; praise the name of the Lord.

All: Blessed be the name of the Lord from this time on and forevermore.

One: From the rising of the sun to its setting the name of the Lord is to be praised.

All: The Lord is high above all nations, and his glory above the heavens.

Collect

God of glory, God of power, we are thankful that you never forget the needy and the poor, and that they are closest to your heart. This day we pray that as we gather in worship we might also praise your name by resolving again to serve your people here and around the world where need is greatest and where things seem darkest. We thank you. We praise you. Amen.

Prayer Of Confession

Lord, we lift up our leaders today, those who deserve our respect and those who do not. Soften hearts that are hardened, lend support to resolve what is wavering, bless those leaders we admire and those we do not. All are your children, all bear a burden, and none of us are worthy. Amen.

Hymns

There Is A Place Of Quiet Rest
Oh, Have You Not Heard?
Sent Forth With God's Blessing

Proper 20/Ordinary Time 25
Sunday between September 18 and September 24 inclusive

Gospel Lesson: Luke 16:1-13
Theme: Follow The Money

Call To Worship (1 Timothy 2:5-6)

One: For there is one God; there is also one mediator between God and humankind, Christ Jesus, himself human,

All: who gave himself a ransom for all — this was attested at the right time.

Collect

This is the day that you have made, Lord! We rejoice and are glad for your lessons and your love. Amen.

Prayer Of Confession

Let the redeemed of the Lord say so! Let God's people show the same love and respect for each other that we see so clearly in the world around us. We are not better than the world. We are saved, and you desire we share this salvation with all. Let us begin this day by treating your people with the respect and dignity all deserve. Silence our lips if gossip rises. Quiet our hearts if resentment surfaces. Still our feet if our desire is to seek out another in order to share criticism. Your Son made it clear that the children of the world know how to treat each other. Allow us to learn from them. Amen.

Hymns

With Happy Voices Singing
O Perfect Love
Bringing In The Sheaves

Proper 21/Ordinary Time 26
Sunday between September 25 and October 1 inclusive

First Lesson: Jeremiah 32:1-3a, 6-15
Theme: The Long Term

Call To Worship

Give thanks to the Lord, all you people. Give thanks to the Lord, all lands. God grants us a future where the world sees none. Pack yourself a suitcase. We're going places. Together.

Collect

With grateful hearts we praise your name. With hopeful spirits we sing your story. With willing hands we work for your kingdom. We come together this morning to strengthen our resolve to take your gospel into a hurting world. Amen.

Prayer Of Confession (built around Matthew 26:39)

One: And going a little farther, (Jesus) threw himself on the ground and prayed, "My Father, if it is possible, let this cup pass from me; yet not what I want but what you want."

All: People of God, hear God's warning — the cup may yet pass from us. Let us claim God's redemption.

Hymns

Glorious Things Of Thee Are Spoken
Steal Away
Here In This Place

Proper 21/Ordinary Time 26
Sunday between September 25 and October 1 inclusive

Second Lesson: 1 Timothy 6:6-19
Theme: A Few Of My Favorite Things

Call To Worship

One: First things first.

All: Pursue righteousness, godliness, faith, love, endurance, gentleness (1 Timothy 6:11).

One: Last things last.

All: For the love of money is a root of all kinds of evil, and in their eagerness to be rich some have wandered away from the faith and pierced themselves with many pains (1 Timothy 6:10).

One: Always remember.

All: If we have food and clothing, we will be content with these (1 Timothy 6:8).

One: Never forget.

All: For we brought nothing into the world, so that we can take nothing out of it (1 Timothy 6:7).

One And All: Fight the good fight of the faith; take hold of the eternal life, to which you were called and for which you made the good confession in the presence of many witnesses (1 Timothy 6:12).

Collect

Lord, so many distractions, some of them blessed. Lord, so many disturbances, some of them terrible. From you, however, comes true peace, true happiness, true joy. As we struggle to chart a course through a world filled with blessedness and terror, we call upon you as our guiding light, and your word as a lamp unto our feet. Bless us in our worship today so we may go forth with full assurance of your presence and your power. Amen.

Prayer Of Confession

Lord, we give back to you that which was always yours. We surrender not only a portion of our wealth, but the idolatry of our materialistic culture. We pledge to turn our eyes away from what we have to what the world needs, and our hearts from what we want to what your kingdom demands. We thank you for this time of giving. Amen.

Hymns

Praise To The Lord, The Almighty
A Charge To Keep I Have
Thou Art The Way

Proper 21/Ordinary Time 26
Sunday between September 25 and October 1 inclusive

Gospel Lesson: Luke 16:19-31
Theme: Pay Close Attention

Call To Worship (based on Psalm 91)

One: You who live in the shelter of the Most High, who abide in the shadow of the Almighty, will say to the Lord, "My refuge and my fortress; my God, in whom I trust."

All: For he will deliver you from the snare of the fowler and from the deadly pestilence; he will cover you with his pinions, and under his wings you will find refuge; his faithfulness is a shield and buckler.

One: You will not fear the terror of the night, or the arrow that flies by day, or the pestilence that stalks in darkness, or the destruction that wastes at noonday.

All: A thousand may fall at your side, ten thousand at your right hand, but it will not come near you.

One: Because you have made the Lord your refuge, the Most High your dwelling place, no evil shall befall you, no scourge come near your tent.

All: For he will command his angels concerning you to guard you in all your ways. On their hands they will bear you up, so that you will not dash your foot against a stone.

One: Those who love me, I will deliver; I will protect those who know my name. When they call to me, I will answer them; I will be with them in trouble, I will rescue them and honor them.

All: With long life I will satisfy them, and show them my salvation.

Collect

Day by day, dear Lord, three things we pray: to see thee more clearly, love thee more dearly, and follow thee more nearly, day by day. Amen. — Richard of Chichester (c. 1197-1253)

Prayer Of Confession

Lord, we hear your promises, but in our midst there is pain and suffering when life is cut short. We struggle with the contradictions between what we read in your scriptures and what we observe in our lives. But we know that with you all will be well, and all manner of things will be well. If we cannot always hear your answer, allow us to feel your presence in your midst. When we live the rich life you have promised us as disciples, then every day can be as a thousand years, and we become every bit as strong as your heroes of old. Hear our prayer. Draw us closer together as your disciples and your people. Amen.

Hymns

Morning Has Broken
All People That On Earth Do Dwell
Wonderful Grace Of Jesus

Proper 22/Ordinary Time 27
Sunday between October 2 and October 8 inclusive

First Lesson: Lamentations 1:1-6
Theme: The Real 9/11

Call To Worship

Oh, people, let us come together, mindful of misery but also of hope.

Collect

Lord, we know you uphold the righteous. We know that the heritage of the blameless will abide forever. But there are times when it seems that your justice is delayed. Grant us patience. Grant us the wisdom and courage to abide as your faithful people, while we wait for the vindication that will come with your Son's return. Though we stumble, we know we shall not fall headlong, for you hold us by the hand. You remain our refuge. You remain our strength. Fashion our worship so that we are more perfectly made in your image through the time we spend together. Amen.

Prayer Of Confession

God of history, we confess that we have focused on our own wounds, which are real enough, and have ignored the true measure of suffering the world over. We have used ourselves as the measure of misery, not as your beloved children who have experienced depths we cannot even imagine. We turn from the idolatry of self-worship and see the world through your eyes. Grant us hope and allow us to be the bearer of that hope to others. Amen.

Hymns

By The Waters
Babylon Streams Received Our Tears
Where You There?

Proper 22/Ordinary Time 27
Sunday between October 2 and October 8 inclusive

Second Lesson: 2 Timothy 1:1-14
Theme: Our Blessed Past, Our Hopeful Future

Call To Worship

We put our trust in God. Praise the Lord! Precious Lord, lift us up!

Collect

God of our past, Spirit who lives in us today, dwell richly among us in all the generations we share. Amen.

Prayer Of Confession

We thank you, Lord, for those whose very life is a confession of faith, whose children are not determined by blood type or DNA, but by the disciples they have drawn to you through word and deed. They are the pattern of your sound teaching, and the assurance that your Spirit is at work among us. Inspire us to follow in their footsteps, faithful to your teachings, sensitive to the needs of the world around us. Amen.

Hymns

God Of Grace And God Of Glory
Faith Of The Martyrs
We Walk By Faith And Not By Sight

Proper 22/Ordinary Time 27
Sunday between October 2 and October 8 inclusive

Gospel Lesson: Luke 17:5-10
Theme: Pass The Mustard

Call To Worship (based on Psalm 37)

One: Trust in the Lord, and do good.
All: Take delight in the Lord, and he will give you the desires of your heart.
One: Commit your way to the Lord; trust in him, and he will act.
All: He will make your vindication shine like the light, and the justice of your cause like the noonday.
One: Be still before the Lord, and wait patiently for him.
All: Yet a little while, and the meek shall inherit the land, and delight themselves in abundant prosperity.

Collect

Our children we sanctify for you. These hearts we set aside for you. These moments we return in thankfulness to you. Our living is part of our worship and praise. You are our example in this and all things. Amen.

Prayer Of Confession

This day, O Lord, and every day, we seek to be your visible people upon the earth. We seek to make your glories known through our actions. Bless us in our time of sharing. Hear our prayers. Where there is sorrow, grant comfort. Where there is despair, grant hope. Where there is joy, grant that we all share in that joy. Where there is sickness, grant healing. Where there is celebration, let others hear our praise of you. This day, every day, let us be your people, wherever we might gather, knowing that whatever place we may be found, there you are in our midst. Amen.

Hymns

Ask Ye What Great Thing
My Faith Looks Up To Thee
We Walk By Faith

Proper 23/Ordinary Time 28
Sunday between October 9 and October 15 inclusive

First Lesson: Jeremiah 29:1, 4-7
Theme: Make Yourself At Home

Call To Worship

God has given us a good home, not made with human hands, but the world that surrounds us, sustains us, and despite our best efforts to destroy it, yet endures. Seek the welfare of this planet where you have been planted, and make yourself at home, here in this sanctuary, and here in this world.

Collect

This world is still my home, though I am passing through.
My God whose kingdom's still to come wants us to serve him, too.
The beauty of the spring, the silence of the fall,
The bounty of the summer calls to mind his kingdom hall.

This world is still my home. When winter snowstorms camp
Upon the hillsides white and stark so horses stamp and champ
I celebrate the love that promises us yet more —
We've got a home on earth for now and heaven evermore.

Prayer Of Confession

Gracious Lord, we have demonized the people who share this world with us. We have turned our back on your cities, and set our eyes so firmly on heaven that we have ignored your bounties here on earth, allowing species to be destroyed and resources degraded. We know your Son is coming back, the heir of all things, and that he has a right to expect that we have been good stewards. If there is still time, Lord, we once more dedicate our lives to the service of your people and your world. Amen.

Hymns

This Is My Father's World
A Hymn Of Creation *(see page 271)*
I Sing The Mighty Power Of God

Proper 23/Ordinary Time 28
Sunday between October 9 and October 15 inclusive

Second Lesson: 2 Timothy 2:8-15
Theme: If, Then, Therefore

Call To Worship

Count on it — God will not forget us. God has made us, God pleads with us, God restores us! The saying is sure — God remains faithful! Great is your faithfulness! May our own mirror yours.

Collect

Lord, this is a day we give you thanks and praise for your majesty as it is revealed in the world around us, as well as it is in the faces who return our smile this morning. Grant us your vision as we seek to fulfill your will for our lives as individuals, and as the church you consider precious, a pearl of great price. We proclaim your name Holy, and your Spirit just. Amen.

Prayer Of Confession

There is no God like you, Heavenly Father. We confess today that you are Lord of our lives by right and because of your endless bounty and grace. Amen.

Hymns

Great Is Thy Faithfulness
Sanctuary
Hear Us Now, O God Our Maker

Proper 23/Ordinary Time 28
Sunday between October 9 and October 15 inclusive

Gospel Lesson: Luke 17:11-19
Theme: Good Odds Or Bad Odds

Call To Worship (Psalm 111)

One: Praise the Lord! I will give thanks to the Lord with my whole heart, in the company of the upright, in the congregation.

All: Great are the works of the Lord, studied by all who delight in them.

Left Side: Full of honor and majesty is his work, and his righteousness endures forever.

Right Side: He has gained renown by his wonderful deeds; the Lord is gracious and merciful.

Women: He provides food for those who fear him; he is ever mindful of his covenant.

Men: He has shown his people the power of his works, in giving them the heritage of the nations.

Younger: The works of his hands are faithful and just; all his precepts are trustworthy.

Older: They are established forever and ever, to be performed with faithfulness and uprightness.

One: He sent redemption to his people; he has commanded his covenant forever. Holy and awesome is his name.

All: The fear of the Lord is the beginning of wisdom; all those who practice it have a good understanding. His praise endures forever.

Collect

Lord, we will give thanks to you with our whole heart, in the company of this congregation. Great are your works. We delight in our study of them. Your work is full of honor and majesty and your righteousness endures forever. Bless our gathering this morning, bless us in our praise of you. Lord, you are gracious and merciful. Share your grace with us. Demonstrate your mercy in your continued blessings. The work of your hands is faithful and just. Let your work be manifest in our fellowship as you perfect us in your love. Amen.

Prayer Of Confession (2 Timothy 2:11-13)

One: The saying is sure: If we have died with him, we will also live with him;

All: if we endure, we will also reign with him; if we deny him, he will also deny us;

One: if we are faithless, he remains faithful — for he cannot deny himself.

Hymns

Give Thanks With A Grateful Heart
Lord Of Light, Your Name Outshining
Come, Thou Font Of Every Blessing

Proper 24/Ordinary Time 29
Sunday between October 16 and October 22 inclusive

First Lesson: Jeremiah 31:27-34
Theme: No More Sour Grapes

Call To Worship

Look! This is the real deal! There is a new covenant. There is a new life. Walk into the light.

Collect

We thank you, Father, for new beginnings. We praise you for your grace that calls us once more into covenant, new covenant, new life. Amen.

Prayer Of Confession

God has written the new covenant on our hearts. Let us open our hearts and read for ourselves. Amen.

Hymns

New Earth, Heavens New
Come, Ye Thankful People, Come
This Is A Day Of New Beginnings

Proper 24/Ordinary Time 29
Sunday between October 16 and October 22 inclusive

Second Lesson: 2 Timothy 3:14—4:5
Theme: The Other 3:16

Call To Worship (based on 2 Timothy 3:14-17)

One: Today we gather as your people and call to mind the words of your servant Paul

All: when he wrote from prison to Timothy and said —

Men: but as for you, continue in what you have learned and firmly believed, knowing from whom you learned it,

Women: and how from childhood you have known the sacred writings that are able to instruct you for salvation through faith in Christ Jesus.

Right Side: All scripture is inspired by God and is useful for teaching, for reproof, for correction, and for training in righteousness,

Left Side: so that everyone who belongs to God may be proficient, equipped for every good work.

Collect

Lord, your words are a guide to us, a light in dark places, a lamp on the hidden paths of our lives. Your Word is a gift, which is new every day, rewritten by the Spirit on our hearts so that new meaning and old interpretations mix and melt together, making it possible for us to discern your will for us. As we gather to praise you, worship you, adore you, let our thoughts be guided by the inspiration of your creation visible and invisible around us, the comfort of your presence in your risen Son and your living Word, and the constant action of your abiding Spirit, that we may magnify your name and tell your story to all the nations. Guide us today and every day. Amen.

Prayer Of Confession (From 2 Timothy 4:2)

Let us proclaim the message; be persistent whether the time is favorable or unfavorable; convince, rebuke, and encourage, with the utmost patience in teaching.

Hymns

Thy Word
The Church's One Foundation
In The Rifted Rock I'm Resting

Proper 24/Ordinary Time 29
Sunday between October 16 and October 22 inclusive

Gospel Lesson: Luke 18:1-8
Theme: Don't Give Up So Easily

Call To Worship (based on Psalm 121)

Children: I lift up my eyes to the hills — from where will my help come?

All: My help comes from the Lord, who made heaven and earth.

Children: The Lord is our keeper.

All: The Lord will keep your going out and your coming in from this time on and forevermore.

Collect

Lord, we follow you not because it is easy, but because it requires thought and effort to discern our priorities in this world. We pray that our lives will be used by you to your glory and honor. Bless us in our time of worship. Amen.

Prayer Of Confession

Keep us mindful, Lord, throughout the week of these concerns and joys shared by our sisters and brothers. Let these things be on our hearts and in our heads day by day. We humbly ask that you grant our requests, that you hear our concerns, that you inspire us to be your living presence in the world today. Lord, these things we pray in your name. Amen.

Hymns

Where Cross The Crowded Ways
Holy, Holy, Holy
Take My Life

Proper 25/Ordinary Time 30
Sunday between October 23 and October 29 inclusive

First Lesson: Joel 2:23-32
Theme: God's Spirit On All

Call To Worship (based on Psalm 65)

One: Praise is due to you, O God, O you who answer prayer!

All: Happy are those whom you choose and bring near to live in your courts. We shall be satisfied with the goodness of your house, your holy temple.

Women: By awesome deeds you answer us with deliverance, O God of our salvation; you are the hope of all the ends of the earth and of the farthest seas.

Men: Those who live at earth's farthest bounds are awed by your signs; you make the gateways of the morning and the evening shout for joy.

Women: You visit the earth and water it, you greatly enrich it; the river of God is full of water; you provide the people with grain, for so you have prepared it.

Men: You crown the year with your bounty; your wagon tracks overflow with richness.

Women: The pastures of the wilderness overflow, the hills gird themselves with joy,

Men: meadows clothe themselves with flocks, the valleys deck themselves with grain, they shout and sing together for joy.

All: For this reason we praise you, and seek to honor you through our obedience.

Collect

Lord, it is our intent this morning to bless you as you have blessed us. Call us to the work of your kingdom. Let your will be done now and always. Yours is the glory, forever and ever. Amen.

Prayer Of Confession

God will give back the years we have lost, now or forever. Let us all, as sinners, turn back to the Lord. Then God's Spirit will rest on all of us, sons and daughters, young and old. Amen.

Hymns

Rejoice, The Lord Is King!
Dona Nobis Pacem
Open My Eyes, That I May See

Proper 25/Ordinary Time 30
Sunday between October 23 and October 29 inclusive

Second Lesson: 2 Timothy 4:6-8, 16-18
Theme: Finish Line

Call To Worship

Let us run the good race, let us continue faithfully to the finish line!

Let us keep the faith — not just for the crown that waits for us, but for the king who deserves no less from us. Let us gather together to worship and praise the Most High.

Collect

Father of all, we come prepared to stand up for all, that none of your children shall be marginalized, abandoned, or ignored. Amen.

Prayer Of Confession

Your servant, Paul, felt abandoned by all but a few, but he knew you would not forsake him. May our faith be as strong so we might confess you as Lord and Savior no matter what the consequences. Be merciful to us, Lord of life. Amen.

Hymns

There Is A Place Of Quiet Rest
Just As I Am
You Shall Go Out With Joy

Proper 25/Ordinary Time 30
Sunday between October 23 and October 29 inclusive

Gospel Lesson: Luke 18:9-14
Theme: Last First, First Last, Always

Call To Worship

God will grant justice. Share in the justice. Share in the joy. Come, now is the time to worship.

Collect

Lord, we say that we are yours, yet even as we gather, our minds are distracted by the small and large things that have happened to us, as well as by our plans for later today and later this week. We are your imperfect people in our gathering. Still our hearts and focus our minds upon our worship, as we seek to call to mind not only your many blessings, but your glory, which is perfect and your kingdom, which is peace itself. Honor our intentions, Lord, more than our actions. We seek to become your will, to be truly yours, as individuals and as your people. We praise you this day. Amen.

Prayer Of Confession (Luke 18:13)

(Unison) God, be merciful to me, a sinner!

Hymns

Come, Now Is The Time To Worship
Simple Gifts
Open, Lord My Inward Ear

Proper 26/Ordinary Time 31
Sunday between October 30 and November 5 inclusive

First Lesson: Habakkuk 1:1-4; 2:1-4
Theme: In Letters Big Enough To Read

Call To Worship (based on Habakkuk 2:1-4)

One: I will stand at my watchpost, and station myself on the rampart;

All: I will keep watch to see what he will say to me, and what he will answer concerning my complaint.

Right Side: Then the Lord answered me and said: Write the vision;

Left Side: make it plain on tablets, so that a runner may read it.

Women: For there is still a vision for the appointed time; it speaks of the end, and does not lie.

Men: If it seems to tarry, wait for it; it will surely come, it will not delay.

All: Look at the proud! Their spirit is not right in them, but the righteous live by their faith.

Collect (prayer for offering)

Today we lay at the altar the gifts of our wealth, our caring, our intentions, and our faith. Use these gifts for the work of your kingdom. Guide us as faithful stewards in this great work. Then it might truly be said of us, today salvation has come to our house! Amen.

Prayer Of Confession

Lord, we watch and wait for the coming of our king. We wait, and certainly it seems that you tarry. Yet you have promised that all good things will happen in your time. We live by our faith, or at least that is our claim. This day, purge us of all pride and create us as your humble servants. Fill our hearts with your vision, and live within us so brightly that even those who rush by us will be able to plainly read your message of hope and salvation through our words and our lives. Let all we do reveal your glory! Amen.

Hymns

This Is The Day That The Lord Has Made
No Night There
God Is Working His Purposes Out

Proper 26/Ordinary Time 31
Sunday between October 30 and November 5 inclusive

Second Lesson: 2 Thessalonians 1:1-4, 11-12
Theme: Real Churches Get Heat

Call To Worship

(based on Job 19:23-25 and 2 Thessalonians 2:15-17)

One: Let us gather to worship, echoing the words of Job in his affliction ...

All: "O that my words were written down! O that they were inscribed in a book!

Men: O that with an iron pen and with lead they were engraved on a rock forever!

Women: For I know that my Redeemer lives, and that at the last he will stand upon the earth...."

One: Clinging to God's promise of a Redeemer, we call to mind the words of the Apostle Paul:

All: So then, brothers and sisters, stand firm and hold fast to the traditions that you were taught by us, either by word of mouth or by our letter.

Men: Now may our Lord Jesus Christ himself and God our Father, who loved us and through grace gave us eternal comfort and good hope,

Women: comfort your hearts and strengthen them in every good work and word.

One: Let us pray.

Collect

We praise you, Lord, for the wonder of your salvation, which is all around us, for your Spirit that moves in our midst, for your creation which provides the foundation of our security. In the midst of adversity we proclaim that our Redeemer lives. Comfort our hearts and strengthen them in every good work and deed. Help us to stand firm and hold fast to what we have been taught by word of mouth or letter. Grant us a clear vision of our Lord Jesus Christ, that we may proclaim your eternal comfort and good hope. Bless us in our gathering today, and in our going hence. These things we pray in the name of this risen Lord. Amen.

Prayer Of Confession

Today we pray for your persecuted church — not us. We whine, we moan about those minor inconveniences that come from living in a free and multicultural society, but we know nothing of the persecution, the pain, the isolation, the imprisonment, the fear, that our brothers and sisters know around the world in lands where it is more than a word to say we have taken up our cross to follow you. We pledge to do more than stand in solidarity with our sisters and brothers — with the help of your Holy Spirit we hope to reach out to them. Soften the hearts of their leaders and bring closer the day when we may all worship in freedom. Amen.

Hymns

I Know That My Redeemer Lives
Savior Of My Soul *(see page 282)*
Children Of The Heavenly Father

Proper 26/Ordinary Time 31
Sunday between October 30 and November 5 inclusive

Gospel Lesson: Luke 19:1-10
Theme: What's It Worth To Ya?

Call To Worship

Some people around the world are willing to do anything to see Jesus. Today you have proven willing at the least to rise from comfort to find this church! How much farther are we willing to go together to see our Lord? Come!

Collect

Lord, give us the courage through our worship to do your will this day and every day, in all our acts of giving and kindness, in all our intentions of heart and spirit. Amen.

Prayer Of Confession

Lord, we long for your presence among us. And we forget you are present, not only through the constant action of your Holy Spirit, but through the abiding presence of your people. We claim to be your people. Open our hearts to the needs around us, here in this place, and around the world. We intend to bear each other's burdens. With your help and encouragement this will be so. Bless us in the hearing of joys and concerns, both spoken and unspoken. Live in our lives together, O Lord. Amen.

Hymns

Come, Thou Font Of Every Blessing
Wonderful Word Of Life
Take My Hand And Lead Me Father

Proper 27/Ordinary Time 32
Sunday between November 6 and November 12 inclusive

First Lesson: Haggai 1:15b—2:9
Theme: You Ain't See Nothin' Yet!

Call To Worship (Psalm 19:1-9)

One: The heavens are telling the glory of God; and the firmament proclaims his handiwork.

All: Day to day pours forth speech, and night to night declares knowledge.

One: There is no speech, nor are there words; their voice is not heard;

All: yet their voice goes out through all the earth, and their words to the end of the world. In the heavens he has set a tent for the sun,

One: which comes out like a bridegroom from his wedding canopy, and like a strong man runs its course with joy.

All: Its rising is from the end of the heavens, and its circuit to the end of them; and nothing is hid from its heat.

One: The law of the Lord is perfect, reviving the soul; the decrees of the Lord are sure, making wise the simple;

All: the precepts of the Lord are right, rejoicing the heart; the commandment of the Lord is clear, enlightening the eyes;

One And All: the fear of the Lord is pure, enduring forever; the ordinances of the Lord are true and righteous altogether.

Collect

Lord we put our house in order as we prepare for the coming of the king. Even now we are surrounded by reminders of a holy day which becomes so full with activities it is no longer a holiday. We thank you and praise you for this time set apart to worship you, and we pray that the service we offer you today and throughout the week will help us as we approach a time of high expectations and high stress.

Though we prepare to mark once more the birth of your Son we proclaim to the world that Jesus reigns! Christ is alive. Together we praise you in word and song. Amen.

Prayer Of Confession (Psalm 19:14)

(Unison) Let the words of my mouth and the meditation of my heart be acceptable to you, O Lord, my rock and my redeemer.

Hymns

Christ Is Alive, Let Christians Sing!
What Is This Place?
The Little Brown Church In The Dale

Proper 27/Ordinary Time 32
Sunday between November 6 and November 12 inclusive

Second Lesson: 2 Thessalonians 2:1-5, 13-17
Theme: First Tomato, First Apple, First Fruits

Call To Worship (Psalm 17:1-6)

Hear a just cause, O Lord; attend to my cry; give ear to my prayer from lips free of deceit.

From you let my vindication come; let your eyes see the right.

If you try my heart, if you visit me by night, if you test me, you will find no wickedness in me; my mouth does not transgress.

As for what others do, by the word of your lips I have avoided the ways of the violent.

My steps have held fast to your paths; my feet have not slipped.

I call upon you, for you will answer me, O God; incline your ear to me, hear my words.

Collect

Lord, you have made known your victory. As the first fruits of your harvest may we make plain through our brokenness that your strength makes all things possible to a hurting world. Amen.

Prayer Of Confession

We offer to you the fruits of our discipleship, to you their author, with joyful and glad hearts. Bless us as we dedicate ourselves to your work in this world. Amen.

Hymns

Morning Has Broken
Come, Ye Thankful People, Come
Now Thank We All Our God

Proper 27/Ordinary Time 32
Sunday between November 6 and November 12 inclusive

Gospel Lesson: Luke 20:27-38
Theme: Smart Aleck Questions, Smart Answers

Call To Worship (Psalm 98)

O sing to the Lord a new song, for he has done marvelous things. His right hand and his holy arm have gotten him victory. The Lord has made known his victory; he has revealed his vindication in the sight of the nations. He has remembered his steadfast love and faithfulness to the house of Israel. All the ends of the earth have seen the victory of our God. Make a joyful noise to the Lord, all the earth; break forth into joyous song and sing praises. Sing praises to the Lord with the lyre, with the lyre and the sound of melody. With trumpets and the sound of the horn make a joyful noise before the king, the Lord. Let the sea roar, and all that fills it; the world and those who live in it. Let the floods clap their hands; let the hills sing together for joy at the presence of the Lord, for he is coming to judge the earth. He will judge the world with righteousness, and the peoples with equity.

Collect

Hear us today, O Lord, as we make our joyful noise together. We come to you, not to ask for praise for our technical skill in singing, or to impress you with the cleverness of the words we present before you, nor to attract your attention through the clothes we wear or the cars we drive. We come because we are your people and you are our God. It is you who have found us, you who have called us, you who have made us who we are. We raise our voices with all of creation, and with all your people, because the victory is yours and salvation is ours. Amen.

Prayer Of Confession

Gracious Father of all humankind, we have come to you with our concerns and our joys. We pray that you will hear our words, spoken and unspoken, and that your Spirit will work great wonders in this world. We pray also that you will cause us to hear as well, so that we ourselves may take up our cross, our burden, our responsibility, and our privilege, presenting the face of Jesus Christ to others through our words, our actions, and our intentions. You are the Lord of this world, and we are your servants. Set for us our tasks, make our mission clear. Amen.

Hymns

We Have Heard The Joyful Sound
We Walk By Faith
I Am Weak And I Need Thy Strength

Proper 28/Ordinary Time 33
Sunday between November 13 and November 19 inclusive

First Lesson: Isaiah 65:17-25
Theme: Sweeping Changes

Call To Worship (built around Isaiah 65:21-23)

Let us build houses and inhabit them; let us plant vineyards and eat their fruit. Let us not labor in vain. Receive the blessing of the Lord!

Collect

Good and gracious God, we thank you today for the evidence all around us of the faithfulness and hard work of your people! Amen.

Prayer Of Confession

Lord of the garden, God of the fields, you have pledged that we shall in your time reap what is yours, and that all will share the results of hard work and labor. So many labor for others and reap nothing. Workers in sweat shops, virtual slaves in the pastures of plenty, those who labor to feed others around the globe and are paid pennies for what is killing them, this is what angers you, Lord, this is what stalls your kingdom. We have been complacent about the source of our goods and never questioned the means of their manufacture. We have comforted ourselves in our ignorance and satisfied ourselves at their expense. We are one family as you are one God. Their welfare is ours. We confess our sins. We pray for your intervention and our own action. Amen.

Hymns

All Creatures Of Our God And King
For The Beauty
God, Make Us Your Family

Proper 28/Ordinary Time 33
Sunday between November 13 and November 19 inclusive

Second Lesson: 2 Thessalonians 3:6-13
Theme: Idleness Versus Sabbath

Call To Worship

We have come together for the great work of nothing — nothing as far as the world is concerned. We will manufacture nothing, produce nothing, create nothing. But with your presence we will come into possession of everything — without trying, because of your grace.

Collect

Thank you, Lord, for this special day. Let it be your day, a separate day, a holy day, a kingdom day. Amen.

Prayer Of Confession

We have not been idle, we pray, in your service, and if we have come to a well-earned rest it is only with the resolve that we must follow your example and claim our sabbath before returning to your great work. In idleness gossip may flourish. In idleness the idolatry of smugness and false superiority finds fertile ground. In rest and reflection we may through prayer rediscover you, and in being faithful and obedient to your gift of sabbath we may become better equipped for your kingdom. Bless us in our gathering today, separate from the world, set aside for a great purpose. Amen.

Hymns

Morning Has Broken
There Is A Place Of Quiet Rest
Take My Life

Proper 28/Ordinary Time 33
Sunday between November 13 and November 19 inclusive

Gospel Lesson: Luke 21:5-19
Theme: Are You Ready? Are We Ready?

Call To Worship

Rejoice this day in what God is creating. Rejoice in what we see all around us. Christ has died. Christ is risen. Christ will come again!

Collect

Thank you, Lord, for the hope we have in your kingdom, both present and to come. Amen.

Prayer Of Confession

We thank you, Lord, for your words of comfort, for your reminder that the whole world is experiencing the birth pangs of a new creation. Let our joy at the thought of your return be tempered with our concern for all, that all may come to know you and love you, and share in the new creation. Amen.

Hymns

Good Night And Good Morning
Joy To The World
In The Bulb There Is A Flower

Christ The King (Proper 29/Ordinary Time 34)
Sunday between November 20 and November 26 inclusive

First Lesson: Jeremiah 23:1-6
Theme: Raise Up A Shepherd

Call To Worship (based on Psalm 46:1-5, 10)

One: God is our refuge and strength, a very present help in trouble.

All: Therefore we will not fear, though the earth should change, though the mountains shake in the heart of the sea;

One: though its waters roar and foam, though the mountains tremble with its tumult. *Selah*

All: There is a river whose streams make glad the city of God, the holy habitation of the Most High.

One: God is in the midst of the city; it shall not be moved; God will help it when the morning dawns. [And God said:]

All: "Be still, and know that I am God! I am exalted among the nations, I am exalted in the earth."

Collect (Jeremiah 23:5-6)

One: The days are surely coming, says the Lord, when I will raise up for David a righteous branch, and he shall reign as king and deal wisely, and shall execute justice and righteousness in the land.

All: In his days Judah will be saved and Israel will live in safety. And this is the name by which he will be called: "The Lord is our righteousness."

Prayer Of Confession (based on Jeremiah 23:4-6)

Heavenly Father, we call upon you to gather the remnant of your flock and bring us together into one fold. You call upon us to become your shepherds caring for your flock. With you beside us and behind us, we will fear no longer, nor shall we be dismayed. You are our righteousness, you are our peace. You bring us together as one people. As we share in your vision of what your kingdom will be, strengthen us as we strive to mirror your vision in our life together as your disciples. Where there is need, call us to share with each other. Where there is want, open our hearts that we may see and hear the opportunity for ministry. Where there is pain and suffering, hallow our own brokenness so that your strength becomes apparent in our walk together toward healing. This is your kingdom, your fellowship, your church, and your vision. We are your people. Amen.

Hymns

Praise To The Lord, The Almighty
Shall We Gather
Jesus, Lover Of My Soul

Christ The King (Proper 29/Ordinary Time 34)
Sunday between November 20 and November 26 inclusive

Second Lesson: Colossians 1:11-20
Theme: Share In The Inheritance

Call To Worship

Children: Blessed be the Lord God of Israel.
Adults: For he has looked favorably on his people and redeemed them.

Collect

Lord God, we still our hearts, we open our eyes, and wait patiently for your coming, as we approach this life-giving stream that makes glad your city. Let this, our sanctuary, be your holy habitation for a time, and walk with us beyond these walls as we engage in service in your name. Amen.

Prayer Of Confession (Colossians 1:15-20)

[Jesus] He is the image of the invisible God, the firstborn of all creation; for in him all things in heaven and on earth were created, things visible and invisible, whether thrones or dominions or rulers or powers — all things have been created through him and for him. He himself is before all things, and in him all things hold together. He is the head of the body, the church; he is the beginning, the firstborn from the dead, so that he might come to have first place in everything. For in him all the fullness of God was pleased to dwell, and through him God was pleased to reconcile to himself all things, whether on earth or in heaven, by making peace through the blood of his cross.

Hymns

Crown Him With Many Crowns
Sweet Hour Of Prayer
Breathe Upon Us Holy Spirit

Christ The King (Proper 29/Ordinary Time 34)
Sunday between November 20 and November 26 inclusive

Gospel Lesson: Luke 23:33-43
Theme: Anguish And Resolve

Call To Worship (Psalm 46)

God is our refuge and strength, a very present help in trouble.

Therefore we will not fear, though the earth should change, though the mountains shake in the heart of the sea; though its waters roar and foam, though the mountains tremble with its tumult. *Selah*

There is a river whose streams make glad the city of God, the holy habitation of the Most High.

God is in the midst of the city; it shall not be moved; God will help it when the morning dawns.

The nations are in an uproar, the kingdoms totter; he utters his voice, the earth melts.

The Lord of hosts is with us; the God of Jacob is our refuge. *Selah*

Come, behold the works of the Lord; see what desolations he has brought on the earth.

He makes wars cease to the end of the earth; he breaks the bow, and shatters the spear; he burns the shields with fire.

"Be still, and know that I am God! I am exalted among the nations, I am exalted in the earth."

The Lord of hosts is with us; the God of Jacob is our refuge. *Selah*

Collect

Blessed Lord, this is a day like any other day, a gift from you in which we can choose to gather to worship. But we have come to call it the last Sunday after Pentecost, our last Sunday in Ordinary Time. Next Sunday we will begin to consider once again the story of your entrance into history. This day we pledge again to gather to hear your salvation story, which does not change but is ever new. As your people we pray that your Holy Spirit will descend in our midst that we might come to worthily magnify your name through our praises. We lift up our voices, we cry aloud, we confess, we receive, we rejoice. Thank you, Lord. Thank you! Amen.

Prayer Of Confession

Jesus, God in Gethsemane, even as we offer to stand with you in suffering as well as glory, we know that it is just as likely that like your Apostle Peter we will deny you if pressed. All we can offer to you this day is our good intent, and our knowledge that just as you forgave Peter and threw him back into the front lines so we, too, can count on your forgiveness and understanding, as we try once more to be your witnessing people. Amen.

Hymns

He Is Lord
Majesty
Shall We Gather At The River?

Special Days

Reformation Sunday

First Lesson: Jeremiah 31:31-34
Theme: The New In The Heart Of The Old

Call To Worship

Behold, sisters and brothers, God makes all things new. In the heart of the old covenant we find the soul of the new. Take hold of the life that is offered to us, people of God.

Collect

Thank you, Lord, for this worshiping people who share with us our love of the grace that sets us free. Amen.

Prayer Of Confession

Heavenly Father, we praise you for your gospel of grace, and confess that we have clung to the law, especially when it condemns others. We see the mote in another's eye but ignore the log in ours. You are Lord, and no other. We are your servants, who willingly choose grace and salvation for all. Amen.

Hymns

Praise To The Lord, The Almighty
Faith Of Our Fathers
Here I Am, Lord

Reformation Sunday

Second Lesson: Romans 3:19-28
Theme: Rock Solid And Sure

Call To Worship

If all have sinned and fallen short of the glory of God, all are justified by God's grace through his righteousness. Come together to worship God's glory.

Collect

We praise you, Lord, that you have called us out of the wilderness into the circle of your love. Our worship today is offered to celebrate your grace. Amen.

Prayer Of Confession

Let us uphold God's true law through acceptance of our shared salvation through faith in Jesus Christ. Amen.

Hymns

To God Be The Glory
A Mighty Fortress
It Is Well With My Soul

Reformation Sunday

Gospel Lesson: John 8:31-36
Theme: Here's The Key — Let Yourself Out

Call To Worship

Take hold of the truth, sisters and brothers, the truth that will set us free!

Collect

We praise you, God, for truth and freedom, which are found only in you. Amen.

Prayer Of Confession

Heavenly Father, in your family it doesn't matter if we are sons or daughters of Abraham, or a particular church elder. We are set free by your grace, not by our ancestry. You have no grandchildren, Lord, just the truth that sets us free. Hold open the door of the prison we create for ourselves and set us free once more. Amen.

Hymns

A Mighty Fortress
Revive Us Again
This Is The Threefold Truth

All Saints

First Lesson: Daniel 7:1-3, 15-18
Theme: History Class

Call To Worship

Do not fear, people of God. Strange dreams trouble those who love and wealth is given to the things of this world. Though kingdoms fall and statues crumble, God is God.

Collect

Lord God, we praise your name and dedicate to you the memory of our loved ones who are sustained and preserved through your love and promises. As we reflect on those who have witnessed to your name and gone on before us, we also reaffirm our dedication not to their memory, although it is important in our lives, but to you, Lord of history, God of salvation. Amen.

Prayer Of Confession

Lord Jesus, we recognize you in our lives, and in all of history. We see that you have been active in our past, personally and as your people, and thank you that you have made your glory evident to all people in all ages. Ancient of Days, you tell us that kingdoms will rise and fall, and that if we are to give thanks for anything, it is that you sustain us through bad times and good. Let kingdoms fall, even our own. You are God and Lord, and though heaven and earth shall pass away, your Word is eternal. You are the living Word. We are your disciples, your servants, your family. We praise you. We pray these things in your name. Amen.

Hymns

O Where Are Kings And Empires Now?
Give Thanks With A Grateful Heart
Come, Ye Thankful People, Come

All Saints

Second Lesson: Ephesians 1:11-23
Theme: Seal Of Approval

Call To Worship

Let us not cease in giving thanks for each other, and for the salvation that comes from our Lord.

Collect (based on Song of Songs 8:6)

Mark us as your own, set us as a seal upon your heart, O God, for your love is stronger than our death, and your passion to save us more powerful than the terrors of the grave. We give you thanks for our shared destiny, God of glory and power. Amen.

Prayer Of Confession

You have turned our heartache and sorrow to joy, not always by curing, but always by healing. O healing Spirit, transform us, so that your light may shine brightly in our broken lives and saved souls. Amen.

Hymns

O Healing Spirit
We Gather Together
Precious Lord

All Saints

Gospel Lesson: Luke 6:20-31
Theme: Blessings And Woes

Call To Worship (Psalm 32:1-7)

One: Happy are those whose transgression is forgiven, whose sin is covered.

All: Happy are those to whom the Lord imputes no iniquity, and in whose spirit there is no deceit.

One: While I kept silence, my body wasted away through my groaning all day long.

All: For day and night your hand was heavy upon me; my strength was dried up as by the heat of summer.

One: Then I acknowledged my sin to you, and I did not hide my iniquity; I said, "I will confess my transgressions to the Lord," and you forgave the guilt of my sin. *Selah*

All: Therefore let all who are faithful offer prayer to you; at a time of distress, the rush of mighty waters shall not reach them.

One And All: You are a hiding place for me; you preserve me from trouble; you surround me with glad cries of deliverance.

Collect

God of nations, God of history, God of peace, God of hope, we praise you this morning, secure in your love, trusting in your wisdom, and patient in our enduring the tumult of the times. We pray for your guidance upon your people this week, both here in our nation, and among all your children the world over, as we humbly seek your will for our lives. We confess our sins to you and thank you for your steadfast love and mercy. You are our hiding place, our sanctuary from trouble. Surround us with those glad cries of deliverance. We pray today in the name of the Father, the Son, and the Holy Spirit. Amen.

Prayer Of Confession

One: Rejoice in that day and leap for joy,

All: for surely our reward is great in heaven!

One: We celebrate the memory of those who have gone before us, successful in their witness.

All: We share their resolve and hope to be found as worthy and as saved. Amen.

Hymns

Come Let Us All Unite To Sing
Here From All Nations
Take Up Your Cross

Thanksgiving Day

First Lesson: Deuteronomy 26:1-11
Theme: Giving And Receiving

Call To Worship

One: Let us give thanks to the Lord, our God.
All: Let us give God thanks and praise!
One: The Lord is more than good. The Lord is active and involved in history.
All: Let us make kingdom history with our God.

Collect

We give thanks, Lord, for the chance to share our bounty with each other, to receive as well as to give. Amen.

Prayer Of Confession

We are quick, Lord God, to give you thanks for the opportunity to serve others. Teach us how to receive, and to thank you for the opportunity to receive from others. For missionaries from other countries, who come to our shores because of their concern for our spiritual welfare — we give you thanks. For those who are poorer than us economically but richer spiritually, who give to us — we give you thanks. For the prayers offered for our benefit though we suppose that we are in church of our spiritual destiny — we give you thanks. We give you thanks for the chance to receive. Amen.

Hymns

Sing To The Lord Of Harvest
Come, Ye Thankful People
For The Beauty Of The Earth

Thanksgiving Day

Second Lesson: Philippians 4:4-9
Theme: Good Things — Good God

Call To Worship (Philippians 4:8 and 7)

... beloved, whatever is true, whatever is honorable, whatever is just, whatever is pure, whatever is pleasing, whatever is commendable, if there is any excellence and if there is anything worthy of praise, think about these things. And the peace of God, which surpasses all understanding, will guard your hearts and your minds in Christ Jesus.

Collect

Call us once more to rejoicing and thanksgiving for the innumerable blessings you have granted to us. Amen.

Prayer Of Confession

For a people called to rejoice, we can be a pretty glum bunch. We bicker, we fight, we tear each other down. God of joy and wonder, touch our hearts, fill us with the joy that is heaven, the rejoicing that is eternal, so that all who enter our doors will see that surely the presence of the Lord is in this place. Amen.

Hymns

We Gather Together
Surely The Presence
Now Thank We All Our God

Thanksgiving Day

Gospel Lesson: John 6:25-35
Theme: Real Bread — Real Good

Call To Worship

Take hold of the bread of life, and share it with others. We are the body of Christ. The blood has been shed for us. Hallelujah. Give thanks to God.

Collect

Jesus, you have called us to your table and we accept this most holy and most ordinary of invitations. Amen.

Prayer Of Confession

We proclaim the Lord's death until he returns through the breaking of the bread and the drinking of this cup. Amen.

Hymns

Eat This Bread, Drink This Cup
Let Us Break Bread Together
We Plow The Fields, And Scatter

Special Services

A Service For Mother's Day

Call To Worship (based on John 1:1; John 1:14; John 13:34-35)

One: In the beginning was the Word and the Word was with God and the Word was God.

All: God has always been with us, in all we say and think and do.

One: The Word was made flesh and dwelt among us.

All: God's Word was made flesh in Jesus. God's Word is given form in those who love and care for us.

One: God gave us a new commandment, that we should love one another.

All: God's love is made obvious through those whose lives we celebrate on Mother's Day — those who have children as well as those who grow children.

One: And how shall others know we are God's people?

All: All will know we are disciples of Jesus, if we love one another.

Prayer

(Unison) God of love, you gave birth to us, nurtured us, chided us, encouraged us. Like good children we hope we will act according to the example you have given us. This day we pray with your help we'll obey. Amen.

Hymns

God Of Eve And God Of Mary
Surely The Presence
Would You Bless Our Homes And Families?
Faith Of Our Mothers

Children's Benediction

Like a mother, God loves us.

A Service For Hunters

One: We have come to the season of harvest, and have gathered many good things grown in the soil. We come to another season of harvest, and mean to gather together.

Hunters: God called upon us to manage this world for more than just our benefit — God means for us to preserve this heritage for the coming of his Son. We accept our responsibility for every living creature with humility, gratitude, and thanksgiving. We pledge to observe all the rules of safety and courtesy, and to praise your name as we take part in a harvest that benefits the herd and ourselves. We recognize that we have come from dust, and to dust we shall return, that death brings life, and that what comes from the earth belongs to all the people of the earth. We will share the bounty of our harvest with others, we will treat our fellow creatures with respect, we will recognize God in all our comings and our goings.

One: In the first chapter of Genesis we read: Then God said, "Let us make humankind in our image, according to our likeness; and let them have dominion over the fish of the sea, and over the birds of the air, and over the cattle, and over all the wild animals of the earth, and over every creeping thing that creeps upon the earth" (Genesis 1:26). And in the ninth chapter God says to Noah: "Every moving thing that lives shall be food for you; and just as I gave you the green plants, I give you everything" (Genesis 9:3). God has given dominion to humankind over all that is in creation. That dominion is not meant to be a tyranny. God loves this creation and has pronounced it very good. It is God's intention that we live as part of a complex structure, respecting the creatures that share God's world with us. Our Native American brothers and sisters, who lived on this continent long before many others came to these shores, thank those creatures that they hunt for food, and demonstrate their respect for them by using them, not abusing them.

Today we pray for your safety as hunters, and for God's blessing upon your work as stewards of creation. We respect and applaud your commitment to gun safety, and are glad for the fellowship you share with family and friends. In our modern society we have sometimes walled ourselves off from God's creation. We encourage you as you hunt to appreciate the wind and the sun, the cold and the warmth, stately trees and running brooks.

Q: Do you pledge to commit yourself to gun safety, to encouragement of others, to respect for nature, and to wise use of the resources to be found in the deer and other game?

A: We do.

Q: Do you recognize God as the author of all good things, and will you take time for prayer and thanksgiving in all you do?

A: We do.

Congregation: Lord, bless these who come before you today. Guard them, guide them, uphold them. Grant them success according to your will and purpose, and bless all of creation through their actions. These things we pray in your mighty name. Amen.

Pastor: Let us pray.

Heavenly Father, giver of all good, we praise you for the beauty of nature, and for your trust in us, calling upon us to practice good conservation and good sense in all our dealings with nature. Protect and preserve our hunters this season and every season, and let your Spirit fill them with a new awareness of all your glory which is arrayed about us. These things we pray in your Son's name. Amen.

Additional Prayers And Hymns

Prayers For Peace

One: Lord, we come before you humbly, without all the answers, but trusting in your goodness and sure of your wisdom.

All: Lord, we pray for your peace. Not peace as the world knows, but the peace that passes all understanding, that binds our hearts together as one people in love.

* * *

One: Lord we pray for the troops who represent us in troubled spots around the world.

All: Lord, these are the people who speak our language, share this continent, understand our hopes and dreams. These are the people who have left behind loved ones, who now wait and worry over every report of casualties. These are the people we know. Guide their hearts, grant them wisdom, protect them, and bring them home to their waiting families and friends. Shield them from the hatred that can grow in the heart. Grant them peace.

* * *

One: Lord, we pray for the innocent people who dwell in zones of war.

All: For the children, we pray that they will be shielded from the hate preached by others, that they might grow to work for a better and brighter world. For their parents, we pray that work and purpose might be theirs. For all who are innocently caught in the crossfire of bullets, we pray for your presence, your mercy, your peace.

* * *

One: Lord, we pray for those misguided souls who honestly believe they are serving you through violence.

All: We lift up those who believe their own death and the deaths of those they have been taught to think of as enemies is somehow your will. Lord, if their healing is beyond us, it rests in your wisdom, judgment, and mercy. We pray that your Spirit will enter into the hearts of those who may be considering destruction, their own and others' — grant them peace.

* * *

One: Lord, we pray for those who cynically preach hatred, who mislead the young into giving up their lives.

All: God of all, it is your will that none should perish, but that all should have eternal life, yet there is evil in the world, and much of that evil wears a human face. We ask that you perform a mighty work, turning around the hearts and minds of those who hate on a scale that we cannot understand. Let your love reign. Let your mercy put out the fires of hatred that rage the world over, far away and close to home. Grant us peace.

* * *

One: Lord, we pray for ourselves.

All: We confess to you our own hatred, our own fears, our own ignorance. If we have been the cause of anyone's stumbling, deliberately or unwittingly, we confess these things now. Heal us, call us together as your family here in this church, that we might continue to witness to the power and the promise of peace, not peace as the world knows it, but the peace you have brokered through the cross and the resurrection. In the name of Jesus we pray. Amen.

Prayers In Ordinary Times

God of light, God of truth, abide with us as evening falls. The stars shine bright, and you gave them their light. The trees are silvered, and it is you who dress them with the light of the moon. The world is transformed, and yet it is still your earth, your sky, your sea. We are grateful that there is no place we can go that you are not already there. Be with us now as your people gather together in your name. Amen.

* * *

Lord, we know you are present, but we don't share the sense of your presence. Help us to feel that you are walking close beside us during this difficult time. As you led your people through the desert as a pillar of fire by night and as a pillar of cloud by day, help us to see clearly the markers you have placed in our lives, so we may follow you through the dry places of discipleship, and on to the promised land of your kingdom. In Jesus' name we pray. Amen.

* * *

Loving God, we have seen the example of your Son in the multiplication of the loaves and fishes. We know there is enough and even more for us to share, that all may be satisfied. You called for your disciples to aid Jesus in that miracle and you call for us again to call plenty into being again. Help us to become your presence in this world, fulfilling the physical as well as spiritual needs of those in our community as well as around the world. These things we pray in your Son's name. Amen.

* * *

Jesus, as we struggle through disagreements help us to recall that we are all your people, that you have called us into one family, that you are not interested in our squabbles. Help us keep the promise that at your name every knee will bow, as we come together in unity based on your lordship and not our power. Your disciples asked to sit at your right hand, and we ask that that we might prove as worthy if we will seek to be your servants, first and foremost. Bless us with the peace that passes understanding. In your name we pray. Amen.

* * *

God, there is no other but you, no desire as great as the desire to serve you and see you, no longing so deep as the longing in our hearts to be with you and abide by you, no joy so profound except the joy that comes from true apprehension of your works, and no satisfaction greater than when we praise your name. When I recall the works of your hands, in the lives of our ancestors in the faith and in the days of our generation, I proclaim that you are a living God who visits your people in every age, a caring God whose love is felt intimately from the rising to the setting sun, and a saving God, who in the darkest night of our lives abides with us though fast falls the eventide. I will praise you daily, and should I forget to praise, then I beg you to recall to my mind my pledge to you. In Jesus' name we pray. Amen.

* * *

Holy, holy, holy, Lord God Almighty, who are we, a people of unclean lips living in a world of nucleons, to glimpse your glory even from afar in the faces of the human family. Nevertheless we cry aloud, as if fueled by your will, "Here we are! Send us!" Send us into the midst of a tortured land to proclaim the day of your salvation. Send us into a broken people to proclaim that in Christ there is no east or west, in Christ no south or north. Send us through a confused nation to demonstrate through your steadfast love that there is neither black nor white, Asian or Hispanic, native or immigrant, but one people called to the city of God, the pure bride of Christ, descending from the clouds to live in the midst of God's people. You are Lord, and we are your followers. Fill us with your power not for our gain but for the fulfillment of your will. This we pray in your strength. Amen.

* * *

Lord, as nations again feel called to war, as men and women seek to settle their differences through the might of arms, give us the courage to witness now as in the past, that you are the Prince of Peace, that you favor no side, that you love all individuals. You do not know nations or aims or causes. You know us by our name and not by our citizenship. You are not on anyone's side. It is your desire that all come to the cross and stand by your side. If you will give us the strength we will be your witness while passions are strong and reason is weak, calling all again to favor peace and abandon war. Amen.

* * *

Forgiving God, we pray this day for those condemned to die. Whether or not they have committed crimes which shock or grieve us, we acknowledge you as Lord of life and death, and affirm that vengeance is yours, not ours. We call to mind as well the pain and sorrow of family and friends who have lost dear ones as a result of violence, and ask you that comfort survivors even as you have sheltered those who died in pain. What we cannot undo we give to you. What we can change you give to us. Hear our prayer, in our confusion. Fulfill our desire to do your will in a world of ambiguities. Deliver us from darkness and dark desires. Let the least of your children come to you in this hour. For we are convinced that nothing is beyond your forgiving love, and that neither life, nor death, nor angels, nor rulers, nor things present, nor things to come, nor powers, nor height, nor depth, nor any other created things will be able to separate us from the love of God which is in Christ Jesus our Lord. Amen.

* * *

God, this is your world not ours. We thank you for quiet gardens, the first tomato of the season, and the abundant zucchinis in paper sacks. We thank you for fertile fields, abundant corn, and waving grain. Accept our offering to you, which we bring before you, with the resolve that what is yours is only temporarily ours. Let us be worthy in our sharing of this gift you have give to us. Thank you, thank you, thank you, for the renewal of your promise that until the end of time, summer and winter, springtime and harvest, will not cease. Amen.

* * *

Lord, we pray now for the return of your Son and our Savior. We know that Jesus will come at a time of your choosing and not ours, and we will continue to wait patiently as did your servants Simeon and Anna. Nevertheless we reveal to you our heart's desire, that even as we pray your Son will return, that all will confess that Jesus Christ is Lord, that what we have known in part will be known by all in full. We see through a glass darkly. We desire to see you face to face. If it is your will that we wait a little longer, we accept this, but it is our desire to say as God's people, "Now let your servant depart in peace, for our eyes have seen the glory." We pray in expectation of that glorious day. *Maran Atha* — come Lord Jesus. Even so. Amen.

* * *

Lord, what have we forgotten to do? What have we neglected? Who have we ignored? Open our eyes that we may see, open our hearts that we may love, open our ears that we may hear. Let your will become ours. Perfect us in your love. Amen.

* * *

Lord of life, these autumn winds cause leaves to fall, and wake us to the coming of the cold. This is the time of watching signs, departing birds, receding dreams. We know what we wished to do and what we have not accomplished. We call to mind completed tasks. We catalog regrets and carefully shelve for future days those intentions we have fulfilled. All times are yours and all needs you fulfill in their season. Thank you, God, for the animals in their burrows, preparing for deep winter's sleep, and for the life of your people, waiting to be fulfilled in Christ. Lord of lords, God, Light of light, true God of true God. You are what you are. We are your people. This we pray in your Son's name. Amen.

All The World Is Sleeping

(to the tune of "Noel Nouvelet")

All the world is sleeping, buried in the snow.
Branches bare are twining, bending to and fro.
Rivers are chill, joints ache and lose their will.
In the deep of winter, angels bright appear.

All around the noises leave us little room.
Light so bright and cheery can't remove the gloom.
Now's when we need the antidote to greed —
In the deep of winter, angels banish fear.

Lord, amid the bustle, call us to your side,
Let us watch the infant, eyes alive and wide,
Love bats the air, his fingers through the air,
With the sheep and manger, God again is here!

— Frank Ramirez

While All Around The Bells May Ring

(to the tune of "On Jordan's Banks")

While all around the bells may ring
For one day sales or charity,
Here for one hour let us sing
Proclaiming Christ with clarity.

With magnets on the fridge's door
Hang drawings made with childish scrawl
With shepherds, mangers, sheep, and more,
The babe who came to save us all.

And let us pledge to never lose
The wonder that still burns afar.
Ignore distractions. Let us choose
To follow with the kings that star.

Once more the Baptist calls to us,
"Prepare the way through vale and hill!"
Then put aside the season's fuss.
Surrender to the good Lord's will.

— Frank Ramirez

A Hymn For Anointing

(to the tune of Hyfrydol ["Come, Thou Long Expected Jesus"])

Come God's people, be anointed, Claim God's healing balm at last.
Set aside your pride and passion, Christ has fully paid the cost.
All that's fleeting, all that's passing, has its day, then fades away,
But your healing is forever, lasting past the final day.

Come God's people, claim God's pleasure, joys await to those who heed.
Nothing for the self-sufficient, everything to those in need.
Come now forward, and if limping, gladly lean so burdens bear,
Small and great, all harms are healing, if we have a tear to share.

Go, God's people, forth with treasure, not with gold or silver weighed.
With the lamp to light dark places, with the truth that cannot be swayed.
From the manger comes the healer, who upon the cross in scorn
Bore our wounds and brought salvation, born to us on Christmas morn.

— Frank Ramirez

(**Note:** though the third stanza was written for the Advent season the hymn can be used in all seasons, with and without the final verse)

And Did Those Slaves

(to the tune of "Chariots Of Fire")

And did those slaves who tilled the field
Upon this continent of dreams
Still sing their hymns and in their hope
Prove in your love your Spirit will not yield?
And did the workers oft oppressed
Entangled and entwined in schemes
Find in their faith a means to cope
Until their wrongs were some time redressed?

Lord live in all who cry to you
As slaves in Egypt or our land.
Let freedom ring, salvation true,
From eastern shore to western sand.
I will not rest, nor justice lose,
Not while these chariots of fire
Bear prophets safe who still accuse
And confound those who are a liar.

— Frank Ramirez

A Song In Praise Of Freedom

(to the tune of "Come, Thou Font" — Nettleton)

Lord we thank you for our nation,
For this land that makes hearts swell.
And we pray that all creation
Will be dear to us as well.
From the hills that strong surround us
Through the rivers lost to view
And the vistas that astound us —
May these all bring praise to you.

Grant our people strength and vision.
Call our leaders to respect
All who bear the world's derision.
When you come, Lord, to inspect
May you find that we have served you
By our service to your poor.
If our actions have deserved you
Call out more to seek our shore.

Lord, we praise you for the fallen,
Those who faced and conquered fear,
Those who answered at the call, in
You whose name we gladly bear.
Those on distant shore and mountain,
Those who in our midst aver
That your justice that we count on
In equality we share.

Though the backs of slaves were broken
In the building of this land
Still the word of freedom's spoken
Or where silenced, writ in sand.
Freedom riders, teachers, writers,
Suffragettes, in act or song
Against tyranny are fighters,
And we gladly sing along.

May we welcome all those sharing
Freedom's vision who arrive
In our midst, who need our caring.
Let their children grow and thrive.
Let all tongues, on eagle's wing, drum
Out the beat of liberty.
Immigrants all, in your kingdom,
Let our welcome, welcome be.

— Frank Ramirez

A Hymn Of Creation

(to the tune of "Praise To The Lord")

Praise to the Lord, the creator redeemer who found us.
Field and wood, fertile valley, and mountains astound us.
Is it not clear that God in heaven is here
Where his rainforests surround us?

Praise you! Your breath is in each bird and beast who are sharing
Wind, rain, and sea, and the rich loamy earth in our caring.
Sharks in dark seas, or when hive dancing the bees,
In your deep love find their bearing.

People of God, see the bear from deep slumber returning.
Birds build their nests, and the long hidden bulbs flower, burning
Bright in our gaze, in the fair lengthening days
God's love is writ plain for learning.

When you return may this rich gift of globe that you've given
Show that your trust in this task of dominion is proven.
With earth renewed may our best efforts be viewed
As your will done, earth and heaven.

— Frank Ramirez

Awake, My Soul, And With The Sun

("Doxology" — The Album Version)

Awake, my soul, and with the sun
Thy daily stage of duty run;
Shake off dull sloth, and joyful rise,
To pay thy morning sacrifice.

Thy precious time misspent, redeem,
Each present day thy last esteem,
Improve thy talent with due care;
For the great day thyself prepare.

By influence of the Light divine
Let thy own light to others shine.
Reflect all Heaven's propitious ways
In ardent love, and cheerful praise.

In conversation be sincere;
Keep conscience as the noontide clear;
Think how all seeing God thy ways
And all thy secret thoughts surveys.

Wake, and lift up thyself, my heart,
And with the angels bear thy part,
Who all night long unwearied sing
High praise to the eternal King.

All praise to Thee, Who safe has kept
And hast refreshed me while I slept
Grant, Lord, when I from death shall wake
I may of endless light partake.

Heav'n is, dear Lord, where'er Thou art,
O never then from me depart;
For to my soul 'tis hell to be
But for one moment void of Thee.

Lord, I my vows to Thee renew;
Disperse my sins as morning dew.
Guard my first springs of thought and will,
And with Thyself my spirit fill.

Direct, control, suggest, this day,
All I design, or do, or say,
That all my powers, with all their might,
In Thy sole glory may unite.

Praise God, from Whom all blessings flow;
Praise Him, all creatures here below;
Praise Him above, ye heavenly host;
Praise Father, Son, and Holy Ghost.

— Thomas Ken

Pilgrimage Of Faith (Steve Engle and Frank Ramirez)

Steve Engle, a good friend of mine over many decades, and an extraordinarily talented composer and lyricist, received the commission to write "Pilgrimage Of Faith" a couple of years ago. It was meant to commemorate the 100th anniversary of Bethany Theological Seminary, the graduate school for the Church of the Brethren. One day, while working on another joint project, we discussed the nature of the piece and what the lyrics might suggest. Later, Steve asked me for some suggestions on the lyrics. I sent him some poetry I had written when I should have been paying attention during a meeting of our denomination's annual conference.

Steve's music combines the sound of a traditional hymn with a gospel music piece in order to reflect the diversity of our expressions of praise and worship. Though "Pilgrimage Of Faith" was written for a specific occasion, Steve and I also wanted to celebrate the commissioning of all our young people who are choosing to serve the church in many capacities. For that reason, I am including it in this collection.

Pilgrimage of Faith

For the Bethany Theological Seminary Centennial, 2005

ALEXANDRIA 77. 88. - 87. 87. 87. 77

♩=86
[REFRAIN]
G G
1. We will walk the Pil - grim Road
2. & 3. We will walk (We will walk) the Pil - grim Road (Pil -grim Road)
D A7 D7 G
till our feet can walk no more; (Walk no more)
till all hate (Till all hate) — and strife shall cease; (Strife shall cease)
Filled with hope (Filled with hope) — for life to come; (Life to come)
G Gmaj7 G7 C Cm6 G D7
Till we greet our Sav-ior Je-sus and the saints who have gone be
Till we greet (Till we greet) our Sav -ior Je - sus and the world walks the path of
Till we see (Till we see) God's fu-ture ris-ing like a glo - ri - ous shin - ing
G C G
1.& 2. A7 Fm7 Bm7 Gmaj7 A7 D
- fore.
peace. (path of peace)
sun. (shin - ing sun) [To CODA, line 4.]
[To Vs. 1.]
[To Vs. 3.]

*For use with "Pilgrimage of Faith" verses

Text: Frank Ramirez & Steve Engle, 2005
Music: Steve Engle, 2005

Count Well The Cost (Alexander Mack, Sr.)

Alexander Mack, Sr., (1679-1735) was the first minister of the small group that rebelled against the churches of the German states. The Treaty of Westphalia which ended the brutal religious conflict known as the Forty Years' War, mandated that a person belong to the same faith as the local prince. Against this backdrop, eight believers, who had gathered together in Bible study, determined that scripture demanded the following: believer's baptism by adults; anointing for healing; the three-part communion that included Feetwashing, the Love Feast, along with the Bread and Cup; and mutual aid and accountability on the part of the believers. It is said that this hymn was sung by Brethren at their first baptism in 1708 at the Eder River near Schwarzenau, Germany. Since baptism outside the state-sanctioned churches was an act of treason and a capital offense, Mack's hymn called disciples to recall the words of Jesus to "Count well the cost." Mack used his inheritance from his father's mill to support the Brethren until he himself was impoverished. Within 21 years of their first baptism, virtually all of the Brethren had moved to Pennsylvania to escape religious persecution.

The first Brethren hymnal, published in 1720 and rediscovered in the middle of the twentieth century, associated this tune with this text. For more information on Mack and the first baptism see the story "Wading Into Danger," from Frank Ramirez's children's book, *The Meanest Man in Patrick County, and other unlikely Brethren Heroes* (Brethren Press, 2004).

437 Count well the cost

MACH'S MIT MIR 87. 87. 88

1 "Count well the cost," Christ Je - sus says, "when you lay the foun-
2 In - to Christ's death be bur - ied now through bap-tism's joy - ous
3 With - in the church's warm em-brace the child of God is
4 In Chris-tian growth we are ma-tured, of fruit-ful vines a
da - tion." Are you re - solved, though all seem lost, to
un - ion. No claim of self dare you al - low if
mold - ed. God's Spir - it lights the in - fant face and
tok - en. That this good growth may be as - sured oft -
risk your rep - u - ta - tion, your self, your wealth, for
you de - sire com - mun - ion with Christ's true church, his
in God's grace is fold - ed. With child - like steps, Christ's
times to us is brok - en the bread of fel - low-
Christ the Lord as you now give your sol - emn word?
will - ing bride, which, through his word, he has sup - plied.
plan we trace, till we grow up in god - ly grace.
ship re - plete when Christ's re-deemed to - geth - er meet.

Text: Alexander Mack, Sr., *Überschlag die Kost, Geistreiches Gesang-Buch vor alle liebhabende Seelen der Warheit*, 1720;
tr. Ora W. Graber, *European Origins of the Brethren*, 1958, alt.

Music: Johann H. Schein, 1628

Jesus Christ, God's Only Son (Alexander Mack, Jr.)

Alexander Mack, Jr., (1712-1803), the son of the first minister among the Brethren, was well known in the American colonies for his fairness, warmhearted nature, charity, and love. He was also a prolific writer and poet. Born in Germany, he arrived in Philadelphia with his father in 1729. Like all ministers among the Brethren, he supported himself, in his case as a weaver.

Following his father's death in 1735, Mack entered a period of profound depression for nearly ten years, during which he left the Brethren and joined the Ephrata Cloister with their controversial leader Conrad Beissel. After several years, he left the cloister and with two others lived as a hermit in the western frontiers of Virginia, before returning to Germantown, near Philadelphia, and rejoining the Brethren to become one of their greatest leaders. He emphasized that love had to come before simply being correct in doctrinal matters. His epitaph, which he wrote, reads "God, Who us of dust did make / and us again to dust will take — / His wisdom, like the sun, shall break / When in his likeness we wake." The story of his battle against victory over depression, titled "Lost and Found," is also contained in Frank Ramirez's book, *The Meanest Man in Patrick County and Other Unlikely Brethren Heroes* (Brethren Press, 2004).

40 Jesus Christ, God's only Son

PRAISE AND PRAYER 77. 77. 77

1 Je - sus Christ, God's on - ly Son, praise and hon - or
2 Lift, O Lord, thy gra - cious face, give us of thy
3 Bless, O Lord, this church of thine, which thou with thy
be to thee! Thou the great en - thron - ed One,
ho - ly peace. May the light of thy sweet grace
blood didst buy. Fill us with thy grace di - vine;
'round whom throngs of an - gels be. Man - y thou - sand
in our midst, Lord, nev - er cease. Lead thy lambs, we
'twas for us that thou didst die. Thou hast cho - sen
watch - ers there lift up joy - ful praise and prayer.
hum - bly pray, in and out, day aft - er day.
us to be con - se - crat - ed, Lord, to thee.

Text: Alexander Mack, Jr., *Etliche liebliche und erbauliche Lieder*, 1788; tr. Ora W. Garber, *The Brethren Hymnal*, 1951
Music: Nevin W. Fisher, *The Brethren Hymnal*, 1951

Move In Our Midst (Kenneth I. Morse and Perry Lee Huffaker)

This hymn, introduced in *The Brethren Hymnal* (1951) has become the favorite among Brethren. Morse (1913-2001) wrote many hymn texts and served on the committees for two different hymnals. He wrote the first two stanzas of this hymn while working at Camp Harmony in western Pennsylvania. Perry Huffaker (1902-1982) composed the tune while riding with Morse in the back seat of a car on the way to a wedding. Two stanzas were added before its first hymnal appearance.

Morse took pains to encourage Frank Ramirez, and many others, as writers, and the inclusion of this much loved hymn in this book is intended as a tribute to him.

418 Move in our midst

PINE GLEN 99. 99
1 Move in our midst, thou Spir - it of God.
2 Touch thou our hands to lead us a - right.
3 Strike from our feet the fet - ters that bind.
4 Kin - dle our hearts to burn with thy flame.
Go with us down from thy ho - ly hill.
Guide us for - ev - er, show us thy way.
Lift from our lives the weight of our wrong.
Raise up thy ban - ners high in this hour.
Walk with us through the storm and the calm.
Trans - form our dark - ness in - to thy light.
Teach us to love with heart, soul, and mind.
Stir us to build new worlds in thy name.
Spir - it of God, go thou with us still.
Spir - it of God, lead thou us to - day.
Spir - it of God, thy love makes us strong.
Spir - it of God, O send us thy pow'r!

Text: Kenneth I. Morse, 1942, 1949, *The Brethren Hymnal*, 1951
Music: Perry L. Huffaker, 1950, *The Brethren Hymnal*, 1951

Savior Of My Soul (John Naas)

According to the story, John Naas (1671-1741) was cruelly tortured when he refused to join the special guard of the King of Prussia, Frederick William I. When asked by the king why he would not join, he replied, "I have already long ago enlisted ... My captain is the great Prince Emmanuel, Our Lord Jesus Christ." Once freed, he emigrated from Europe to America, where he helped to found the Amwell, New Jersey, congregation. His story is told in the children's book "The Tall Man" by Dorothy Brandt Davis and Carl Brandt Davis (Brethren Press).

The story of the perilous ocean crossing that resulted in a temporary paralysis for Naas is told in "Voyage to Freedom," one of the stories in Frank Ramirez's book, *The Meanest Man in Patrick County and Other Unlikely Brethren Heroes* (Brethren Press, 2004).

549 Savior of my soul

JOHN NAAS 55. 88. 55

1 Sav - ior of my soul, let me choose thy goal. Self to thee I would sur - ren - der, choose thy cross, be thy con - ten - der. Let me choose thy goal, Sav - ior of my soul.
2 Christ, ex - tend thy hand, for I can - not stand. Thy soul's pow'r, O share with me, and I thy fol - l'wer close will be. I am too weak to stand; Christ, ex - tend thy hand.
3 Je - sus, grant me grace so to run my race, that I may vic - to - rious be. Thy fa - vor show and pros - per me. So as I run my race, Je - sus, grant me grace.

Text: John (Johann) Naas, *Heiland meiner Seel'*, *Die Kleine Harfe*, 1792; tr. Lillian Grisso
Music: William Beery, 1944, *The Brethren Hymnal*, 1951

U.S./Canadian Lectionary Comparison

The following index shows the correlation between the Sundays and special days of the church year as they are titled or labeled in the Revised Common Lectionary published by the Consultation On Common Texts and used in the United States (the reference used for this book) and the Sundays and special days of the church year as they are titled or labeled in the Revised Common Lectionary used in Canada.

Revised Common Lectionary	**Canadian Revised Common Lectionary**
Advent 1	Advent 1
Advent 2	Advent 2
Advent 3	Advent 3
Advent 4	Advent 4
Christmas Eve	Christmas Eve
The Nativity Of Our Lord/ Christmas Day	The Nativity Of Our Lord
Christmas 1	Christmas 1
January 1/Holy Name Of Jesus	January 1/The Name Of Jesus
Christmas 2	Christmas 2
The Epiphany Of Our Lord	The Epiphany Of Our Lord
The Baptism Of Our Lord/ Epiphany 1	The Baptism Of Our Lord/ Proper 1
Epiphany 2/Ordinary Time 2	Epiphany 2/Proper 2
Epiphany 3/Ordinary Time 3	Epiphany 3/Proper 3
Epiphany 4/Ordinary Time 4	Epiphany 4/Proper 4
Epiphany 5/Ordinary Time 5	Epiphany 5/Proper 5
Epiphany 6/Ordinary Time 6	Epiphany 6/Proper 6
Epiphany 7/Ordinary Time 7	Epiphany 7/Proper 7
Epiphany 8/Ordinary Time 8	Epiphany 8/Proper 8
Transfiguration Of The Lord/ Last Sunday After Epiphany	The Transfiguration Of Our Lord/ Last Sunday After Epiphany
Ash Wednesday	Ash Wednesday
Lent 1	Lent 1
Lent 2	Lent 2
Lent 3	Lent 3
Lent 4	Lent 4
Lent 5	Lent 5
Sunday Of The Passion/Palm Sunday	Passion/Palm Sunday
Maundy Thursday	Holy/Maundy Thursday
Good Friday	Good Friday

The Resurrection Of Our Lord/Easter Day	The Resurrection Of Our Lord
Easter 2	Easter 2
Easter 3	Easter 3
Easter 4	Easter 4
Easter 5	Easter 5
Easter 6	Easter 6
The Ascension Of Our Lord	The Ascension Of Our Lord
Easter 7	Easter 7
Day Of Pentecost	The Day Of Pentecost
The Holy Trinity	The Holy Trinity
Proper 4/Pentecost 2/O T 9*	Proper 9
Proper 5/Pent 3/O T 10	Proper 10
Proper 6/Pent 4/O T 11	Proper 11
Proper 7/Pent 5/O T 12	Proper 12
Proper 8/Pent 6/O T 13	Proper 13
Proper 9/Pent 7/O T 14	Proper 14
Proper 10/Pent 8/O T 15	Proper 15
Proper 11/Pent 9/O T 16	Proper 16
Proper 12/Pent 10/O T 17	Proper 17
Proper 13/Pent 11/O T 18	Proper 18
Proper 14/Pent 12/O T 19	Proper 19
Proper 15/Pent 13/O T 20	Proper 20
Proper 16/Pent 14/O T 21	Proper 21
Proper 17/Pent 15/O T 22	Proper 22
Proper 18/Pent 16/O T 23	Proper 23
Proper 19/Pent 17/O T 24	Proper 24
Proper 20/Pent 18/O T 25	Proper 25
Proper 21/Pent 19/O T 26	Proper 26
Proper 22/Pent 20/O T 27	Proper 27
Proper 23/Pent 21/O T 28	Proper 28
Proper 24/Pent 22/O T 29	Proper 29
Proper 25/Pent 23/O T 30	Proper 30
Proper 26/Pent 24/O T 31	Proper 31
Proper 27/Pent 25/O T 32	Proper 32
Proper 28/Pent 26/O T 33	Proper 33
Christ The King (Proper 29/O T 34)	Proper 34/Christ The King/ Reign Of Christ
Reformation Day (October 31)	Reformation Day (October 31)
All Saints (November 1 or 1st Sunday in November)	All Saints' Day (November 1)
Thanksgiving Day (4th Thursday of November)	Thanksgiving Day (2nd Monday of October)

*O T = Ordinary Time

WARNING

Removing or tampering with the card on the back side of this page renders this book non-returnable.

Title: Lectionary Worship Aids, Series VII, Cycle C

ISBN: 0-7880-2404-3

INSTRUCTIONS TO ACCESS PASSWORD FOR ELECTRONIC COPY OF THIS TITLE:

The password appears on the reverse side of this page. Carefully cut the card from the page to retireve the password.

Once you have the password, go to

http:/www.csspub.com/passwords/

and locate this title on that web page. By clicking on the title, you will be guided to a page to enter your password, name, and email address. From there you will be sent to a page to download your electronic version of this book.

For further information, or if you don't have access to the internet, please contact CSS Publishing Company at 1-800-241-4056 in the United States (or 419-227-1818 from outside the United States) between 8 a.m. and 5 p.m., Eastern Standard Time, Monday through Friday.